The Lake House at Ramsgate

A Pride and Prejudice Variation
MJ Stratton

The Lake House at Ramsgate
A Pride and Prejudice Vagary
Copyright 2024 by MJ Stratton
Cover design by Pemberley Darcy
All RIghts Reserved

This book is a work of fiction. Any person or place appearing herein is fictitious or is used fictitiously.

All rights reserved, including the right to reproduce this book, or portions thereof, in any form. No portion of this book may be reproduced in any form without written permission from the publisher or author, except as permitted by U.S. copyright law.

NO AI TRAINING: Without in any way limiting the author's exclusive rights under copyright, any use of this publication to "train" generative artificial intelligence (AI) technologies to generate text is expressly **prohibited**. The author reserves all rights to license uses of this work for generative AI training and development of machine learning language models.

This eBook is licensed for personal use only and may not be re-sold or given away to others. If you would like to share this book with another person, please purchase an additional copy for each person. If you're reading this book and did not purchase it, or it was not purchased for your use only, then please purchase your copy.

Thank you for respecting the hard work of this author.

Edited by Ree Hudson

ISBN: 9798340940438

Contents

	V
	VI
About This Book	1
Prologue	3
1. Chapter One	10
2. Chapter Two	21
3. Chapter Three	32
4. Chapter Four	42
5. Chapter Five	51
6. Chapter Six	59
7. Chapter Seven	71
8. Chapter Eight	79
9. Chapter Nine	92
10. Chapter Ten	102
11. Chapter Eleven	112
12. Chapter Twelve	119
13. Chapter Thirteen	128
14. Chapter Fourteen	137

15.	Chapter Fifteen	146
16.	Chapter Sixteen	156
17.	Chapter Seventeen	169
18.	Chapter Eighteen	178
19.	Chapter Nineteen	189
	Epilogue	193
	Other Books by MJ Stratton	201
	Thank You!	202
	Acknowledgements	203
	About The Author	204

For Hannah and Ian

About This Book

In 1812, Elizabeth Bennet, eager for her first visit to the seaside, accompanies her beloved sister Jane and her new brother, Charles Bingley, to Ramsgate. Their retreat, the Lake House, offers an ideal location for Mrs Bingley, whose delicate condition requires rest and care by the sea.

When Jane's condition worsens, Elizabeth steps into the role of mistress of the house, managing the servants, overseeing the menus, and even attending to her brother's correspondence. One letter, intended for the solicitor who arranged the lease, unexpectedly draws a shocking reply from Mr Fitzwilliam Darcy.

Stunned by Mr Darcy's accusations and confused by his claim that it is 1810 and that he owns the Lake House, which he has never leased in his lifetime, Elizabeth responds with sharp, cutting words. As their correspondence continues, it becomes clear that neither has lost their senses; instead, they find themselves caught in a romance that transcends time.

As love blooms, Darcy and Elizabeth resolve to meet, but they soon realise that appearances can be deceiving. Together, they must unravel the mystery of the Lake House and discover who—or what—is conspiring to keep them apart.

Dive into a Pride and Prejudice variation that was inspired by the movie The Lake House. This historical rendition of a fan favorite is sure to thrill the reader!

Prologue

December 1800
Cliff Cottage
Ramsgate

"Come closer, child," the withered old lady said, beckoning her great-grandson nearer. "I am not long for this world and have much to tell you."

The man drew closer, seating himself on a chair beside the bed where his great-grandmother lay, propped up by several down pillows. She was his only remaining family, having outlived her son and grandchildren, and had raised him since his parents' death when he was twelve years old. When his great-grandmother retired, she received a pension and Cliff Cottage, a small but quaint abode by the sea in Ramsgate, near to the Lake House where she had served since she was a young girl.

"I am here," he said quietly, taking her withered hand in his.

"How is your wife?" she rasped. Though her eyes seemed focused on him, they had long since dimmed, and she had been blind for the last five years. "How goes her work at the Lake House?" She chuckled softly. "Bless Fitzwilliam for his childish insistence long ago that it be called *'the'* Lake House. The memory still makes me smile." Young master Darcy had never learned to call the seaside home by its *proper* name.

"Martha is well," he replied with a broad smile. "She felt the quickening only yesterday."

The old woman sighed contentedly. "Then our line will not end with you," she said, her tone pleased. To command his complete attention, she squeezed his hand as tightly as she could manage. "It is vital that it does not end. Our family's purpose—our task—must never fail."

"I do not know what you mean." The man was perplexed, briefly wondering if his grandmother had finally lost her wits. But that thought was absurd. Great-Gran Hannah's memory was as sharp as ever, despite her being nearly five-and-ninety years.

"Your new position at the Lake House will serve you well in the years to come, should your services be required," she continued, ignoring his confusion. "Just as mine served me. It is quite the tale, and knowing you as I do, I would wager you will believe me addled. But I beg you to suspend your disbelief and listen with an open mind."

He nodded, and recalling she could not see him, he promised, "I will do as you ask."

Great-Gran settled back into her pillows. "The Lake House is no ordinary place," she began. "The origin of its unique properties remains shrouded in mystery, and our family's original connexion to it is now lost to time. Yet, since the early 1500s when the first owner built it, someone from our family has always served the family who lived or visited there, which is no small feat."

She paused for a moment to cough, and her companion quickly offered her a drink from the glass on the table beside the bed. Once she quenched her thirst and her throat soothed, she continued.

"The Lake House is a temporal anomaly, a place where the fabric of time is unusually thin. Many of our ancestors have speculated that the location of the house may be the cause, though nothing—or no one—has ever confirmed it to me. The first of our family to serve as steward of the house discovered this peculiar phenomenon when the years 1540 and 1544 collided. His name was Samuel Simmons, and at first, he believed he was losing his sanity. After some initial confusion as he experienced both years simultaneously, Samuel began to unravel what he was witnessing.

"He discovered that, instead of perceiving events as a sequence, he saw the years layered upon each other, like the pages of a book. This unique perspective allowed him to travel through different times within the house as though they were all occurring at once. In his journals, he described moving through the years as akin to walking through different rooms in the same residence, and he noted that the anomaly was restricted within the boundaries of the Lake House. No one else seemed affected by this strange occurrence, and so he kept the knowledge to himself, fearing that others might brand him a sorcerer and burn him at the stake."

The man shifted uneasily in his chair. Great-Gran seemed as lucid as ever, yet the tale she spun was as fantastical as she had implied it would be.

"I can sense your doubt, even from here." Gran chuckled and gestured towards the glass on the table once more. He handed it to her, and she drank deeply. "I was just as skeptical when my father told me the same story. But then, it happened to me."

He stiffened, and she gently squeezed his hand. "Let me finish, and I shall answer your questions afterwards."

"Our ancestors spent many years at the Lake House and discovered that they were given abilities for a specific purpose—to guide and protect those within its walls. Not every member of our line possesses this gift. To exist outside the bounds of time is a profound responsibility the house bestows. In exchange, we are to protect those we serve, lending aid when the house tells us it is necessary."

"When the house tells us?" he repeated. Incredulity coloured his voice, and he shook his head in bewilderment.

"Let me finish," she repeated patiently. She brushed a stray lock of hair from her eyes, expression distant, as if lost in memory. "I was two-and-twenty when I first experienced the phenomena," she continued. "My father related all I now tell you on his deathbed, and, like you, I was skeptical. At the time, I was just newly promoted to housekeeper. The former housekeeper, old Mrs Tilney, trained me as her replacement. My new position came sooner than I had anticipated when she decided to join her daughter in America.

"The Lake family visited every summer. Mr and Mrs Lake delighted in the seaside, and their children were scarcely less enthusiastic. The eldest child, Amelia, was of an age with me, and before my promotion, Mrs Tilney, had assigned me to Miss Lake as her lady's maid. Despite the difference in our respective stations, we became fast friends, often confiding in one another. Miss Lake despaired of ever finding a suitor in town. She had endured four seasons and was unimpressed with the pompous gentlemen she encountered in London. Her dowry was attractive, and she often felt as though she was being hunted rather than courted. But I digress."

Great-Gran sighed, a small smile gracing her lips. "It was a sunny afternoon when the first letter appeared on the salver. I can scarcely describe the feeling—it was as if a string was pulling me closer until I found it. The post had been delivered earlier that day, so it was curious to see a letter waiting there for one of the household. Someone with masculine handwriting had addressed it to *A. Lake*. At first, I assumed it was for the master—he shared initials with his daughter, as you know—but something urged me to place the letter in Miss Lake's hands. I did so and watched as fury descended upon her. I do not know what the letter contained, but she muttered constantly for days about gentlemen importuning her. She penned a reply and bid me place it on the salver.

"As I descended the stairs to carry out her instruction, I noticed an unfamiliar man in the house. His presence would not have been so strange had I encountered him in the public rooms, but he was exiting the master's suite, acting as though he belonged there. He nodded to me as he walked by, and I trailed after him, shocked by his audacity."

Great-Gran grinned mischievously. "He had a newspaper tucked under his arm, and the footman who met him at the door addressed him as *Mr Darcy*. The gentleman dropped the newspaper on the side table in the entrance hall, right next to the salver before he donned his outerwear and left. I went to the table and looked down at the front page, and to my shock, I noted the date was two years in the future. All my father's words to me before he died came rushing back.

"Whilst holding the mistress's letter, I observed that the painting above the Hepplewhite side table was slightly crooked. I reached out to straighten the seascape, but before I could touch it, the painting unexpectedly shifted on its own and fell forward, landing on the table with a heavy thud. I immediately focused on the wall behind it, where a post box, embedded in the wall and previously hidden, became clearly visible.

"My curiosity piqued, I leaned forward and carefully examined the post box. Crafted from rich mahogany, its surface was adorned with intricate carvings of seashells, waves, and starfish—echoes of the nearby coast and the house's connexion to the sea. Oddly, it also had sprigs of lavender carved along its edge. I never did understand why, since there was no lavender anywhere near the Lake House. The painting had concealed the box, even though it was a beautifully made feature of the house, entirely hidden away from prying eyes. As I touched the inside of the box, understanding filled me. It was then I understood that this was no ordinary receptacle. The house itself facilitated these exchanges, and only those who served the house were privy to its secret.

"I placed the letter in the post box, adjusted the painting, and walked away, my mind racing with what I had uncovered. After that, I paid closer attention to the comings and goings in the house. People I had never seen before passed through, and then... my mistress received a reply to her letter just two days later."

Great-Gran paused once more. "You know, of course, that Amelia Lake married Gregor Darcy. I flatter myself by saying that the Lake House and I, as its faithful steward, facilitated their romance. I now pass this responsibility to you. From what family records can ascertain, only *one* of us holds the privilege of navigating the Lake House's temporal intricacies at any given moment. My tenure is nearly at an end, which means you are the next. There is no other."

"How can you believe such nonsense?" the man asked, struggling to keep the derision out of his voice. Great-Gran did not deserve such censure.

"It is as real as you and me," she insisted.

"Why, then, did you wait so long to tell me?" he asked.

"There was always some reason to delay—the death of my son—your grandfather... and then, your parents... But as I grew older, I began to fear that you were not ready, that you needed more time to live your life without the burden of this knowledge. When I retired to Cliff Cottage, I believed the Lake House had finished with me, that my time was truly over, and perhaps the secret could rest as well. Yet the years passed, and as I watched you grow into your own, I realized I could not leave this world without passing on what I knew. I waited because the post box had not yet called to you, and because there had been no pressing need. But now, I feel the time is near. The Lake House will guide you when the moment comes." She grew agitated, and as she sat up, her grip on his hand tightened until it hurt. "Promise me you will do this."

He sought to soothe her. "I promise, Gran," he said. "You may rest easy."

She nodded, her grip loosening as she lay back against her pillows. "Thank you," she whispered. Her eyes closed, and she drifted off to sleep, never to wake.

Chapter One

Lake House
Ramsgate
July 5, 1812
Elizabeth

*D*ear Sir,

    I hope this missive finds you well. My name is Miss Elizabeth Bennet, and I write at the behest of my relations. As requested by the property manager, I have compiled a detailed inventory of the house, its contents, and any repairs deemed necessary upon taking residency. Mr Smythe, the butler, has verified this list.

    Immediately noticeable upon entry are the green tracks of paint—likely left by a cat—marring the steps and the landing. Mr Smythe assures me they have been present for some time and that he can acquire a rug to cover most of the mess.

    Additionally, there is a crack in the glass of the parlour window. Mr Smythe informed me that he ordered a new pane, but he does not expect delivery for another fortnight. The parlour, sitting room, dining room, and music room have no other issues to speak of.

The master's and mistress's suites are in good repair, save for the door that adjoins the rooms. My brother informs me that the handle is broken, and the door will not latch properly. He insists it will be no bother to them, but I record it here, nonetheless.

I reviewed all the furnishings of the house at length, after the staff catalogued them. Everything is in order, and we will conduct another review before we vacate the residence at the end of the lease.

As we have now taken possession of the house, please direct all correspondence here rather than to Netherfield Park.
Thank you for your assistance in seeing us well settled.
Yours, etc.,
Elizabeth Bennet

July 1810
The Lake House
Ramsgate
Darcy

Mr Fitzwilliam Darcy sorted through the post, arranging it into neat piles. There was a letter for Georgiana, several bills, and a letter from his steward. As he neared the bottom of the stack, he frowned. The unfamiliar handwriting caused him to pause, and he examined the missive closely.

The letter had the address of his solicitor in London, Farnsworth-Durham, written on it. The hand was feminine, and he flipped it over to check for a return direction. *E. Bennet, Lake House, Ramsgate.*

What in the world...? Darcy hurriedly broke the seal and unfolded the letter. He skimmed it and then read it again, more slowly. What mischief was this? The Lake House, leased? Preposterous! He studied the letter and noted the date—*July 5, 1812?* How careless of the author of the missive to make such an egregious mistake! With a scoff, he tossed the paper aside. Whomever had sent it was certainly hoping to gain something from him.

Though angered by the presumptuous miss who dared to pen such drivel, his curiosity had taken hold, and he picked the missive up again. Darcy continued to examine the sheet of paper in his hands. It was thick and of good quality, a sure sign that the sender had access to finer things. The writing was elegant, and each line was straight and clean. There were no blots or improperly spelled words, either.

Miss Elizabeth Bennet, he mused. He had never heard of any Bennets; clearly, the author of this bit of fiction was not of the first circles. He searched the letter for any further hint of the lady's identity, and his gaze settled upon the last two sentences. *Netherfield Park.* That was most certainly the name of an estate, which gave him a starting point.

Shaking his head, Darcy wondered what he was thinking? Certainly, it would be more prudent to burn the letter and be done with this nonsense. This Miss Bennet must surely be seeking to entrap him. She had done her research well, disguising a letter to him as one to his solicitor so that she could claim... what?

Frowning, he folded the letter. He pulled a drawer open and stuffed the offensive thing inside, resolving to consider the matter later. A clock chimed somewhere in the house, and he stood, stretching. Tea was to be served shortly, and he was more than ready for it.

Crossing his study in three long strides, he opened the door. The soft tones of the pianoforte drifted through the house, drawing him towards the music room. His fourteen-year-old sister Georgiana sat before the instrument, her tongue between her teeth as she played the same passage again and again. She stumbled over the notes and growled, slamming her hands on the keyboard before closing the lid with a bang.

"Careful, Georgie, lest you damage it," Darcy admonished with mock severity.

His sister sighed. "I cannot get it right," she lamented, folding her arms and sticking her lip out in a pout. "I have been practising all morning, and I continue to make the same error!"

He smothered a smile. Georgiana would not appreciate the humour he saw in the situation. "Perhaps it is time to leave the pianoforte for a while and partake of some tea." He walked towards her and extended his hand. "Come. I have reason to believe that Cook has added lemon tarts to the fare this afternoon."

Georgiana brightened and unfolded her arms to take his hand. Darcy helped her to her feet and escorted her from the music room, walking the short distance down the hall to the parlour where a lovely tea awaited their arrival.

Carefully, Georgiana poured for both of them. Darcy was pleased to see the improvement in his sister's skills. School had been of some benefit to her, despite her frequent complaints about being away from him. Her pleas had not gone unheeded; he had removed her from the establishment for the summer and hoped that she would be ready to return come autumn.

As she ate her lemon tart, Georgiana sighed in pleasure, and Darcy hid another grin. She was very like their mother; Lady Anne Darcy had adored lemon tarts and made no secret of her preference when she partook.

"What say you to a stroll on the beach after tea?" Darcy asked at length. Georgiana nodded enthusiastically, dabbing her lips with her serviette before replying.

"That sounds very agreeable," she said. "I have been inside all day; the cool sea breeze would do me good, I think."

"How have you progressed with your studies today?"

She frowned. "I have finished my French and my history. You heard how my pianoforte practise fared."

Darcy smiled encouragingly at his little sister. "You will master it," he assured her. "There has not been a piece of music yet that you have not conquered."

His flattery succeeded, and Georgiana smiled. "I know. It is only very frustrating that I cannot seem to get the fingering right in that section. Perhaps you can hire a master for me when we return to London in September."

Darcy frowned. "You know you are to return to school in the autumn," he admonished.

Georgiana turned to pleading. "Oh, please, Brother! I beg you not to send me back. School is unbearable! There is nothing taught there that I cannot learn at home!"

"School is not only about learning academics and comportment. It is also about forming connexions and lasting friendships."

"I have connexions aplenty," Georgiana insisted. "Everyone at school is interested in me only so far as learning how to get closer to *you*."

Darcy glanced up from his cup in surprise. "What? You have never said such before. What can you mean by it?"

Georgiana fiddled with the beading on her skirt. She bit her lip and looked up at him. "I tried, Fitzwilliam, I did," she whispered, her voice laced with misery. "Every time I thought I had found a friend, it was only a matter of time before they began asking pointed questions about you. And if it was not about you, they were speaking of their brothers and how eager they would be to introduce me to them. I hated it! By the end of my term there, I kept to myself, only joining the other girls for lessons and meals. If that is what it means to form friendships and connexions, I can do very well without both!"

"Why did you not tell me?"

She sniffed, tears welling in her eyes as Darcy watched. "I thought it was my fault. I thought there was nothing likeable about me. Maybe that was why no one wished to be my friend."

"There is nothing wrong with you, Georgie," Darcy insisted. "Unfortunately, it is the way of our world. People seek connexions and fortune, and often hide their true purposes behind a mask of supposed friendship. My circle is rather small for this reason. I do not have many close friends besides Bingley and our cousin Richard."

"How am I to know whether one's motives are pure or not?"

"Experience will teach you to see through the false characters. It is sad that we must learn by being hurt, but such is life."

Georgiana sipped her tea in silence, clearly mulling over his words. Darcy felt assured that she would gain something from their conversation.

"If you still feel the same way when we return to London, I shall send out inquiries. You will need a companion, and a music master is a necessity."

His sister's spirits lifted considerably. She set her teacup aside and launched herself into his arms. Thankfully, he had set his cup down, and his arms were free to catch her.

"Thank you, Brother!" she cried happily.

Darcy patted her back, and she released him. "Shall we take that stroll on the beach now?" he asked.

She nodded, and the pair returned their teacups to the tray before departing the room. Whilst donning his hat and gloves, Darcy reflected on his conversation with his sister. It was such a pity that young Georgiana learned so soon that even strangers would prevail upon her acquaintance, hoping to create a better situation for themselves. The letter in his desk drawer came again to his mind, and he resolved to pen a reply to the impertinent miss on the morrow.

They spent a pleasant afternoon strolling along the beach. Georgiana found several shells for her collection, adding them to the sack her brother held, which they had brought specifically for that purpose.

"I shall need another bowl soon," Georgiana said to him as she placed a treasure into the sack. She spoke of the large vessel on her bedside table, a considerable-sized container filled with all kinds of things she had collected from the beach over the years.

"I will browse the shops for one tomorrow," her brother promised.

"Are you to visit the village then?"

"Yes."

"Might I come with you?" Georgiana turned pleading eyes towards him, and he smiled affectionately.

"No, you cannot," he said with a grin. "Your presence would defeat my purpose."

Understanding dawned on her face. "Oh! You are looking for something for *me!*"

"Indeed. It is your birthday next week. Fifteen! How quickly the time has flown." His heart tightened. Georgiana had become grown. All too soon, she would make her come out and suitors would swarm around her like bees to a flower. Darcy felt utterly unprepared for such an event. He was grateful that there were still three years until that time.

Georgiana linked her arm through his and squeezed.

"Have you any particular requests?" he asked. Shopping for his sister had been so simple last year. Now, he hardly knew what would please her.

Georgiana considered his words. "A recent novel would be nice. And you must not forget to look for a new treasure bowl."

Darcy breathed a sigh of relief, glad to know Georgiana's simple tastes would make his task much easier. "And should I instruct Cook to prepare anything special?"

"Lemon tarts!" was her instant reply. Her enthusiasm caused him to chuckle, and she playfully swatted his arm.

"I will inform Cook." He gently squeezed her hand and turned back towards the house. They changed for dinner and after a quiet meal and a peaceful evening, he and Georgiana retired.

The next morning, Darcy was back in his study. After completing a letter to his steward and declining several invitations, he retrieved the strange missive out of his drawer for another review. After Georgiana's disclosures at tea the day before, Darcy felt far less willing to burn the letter and simply ignore its existence. He needed to squelch Miss Bennet's attempt at ingratiation as swiftly as possible. A harsh, unyielding reply was in order. With resolve, he pulled a fresh sheet of paper towards him and dipped his quill into the ink pot. He thought for a moment and began to write.

The Lake House
Ramsgate
July 6, 1810

Dear Madam,
I am utterly astonished to have received a letter of this nature from an unknown person. This flagrant attempt at making the acquaintance of the Darcys is beyond the pale. Never have I experienced such a display! I inform you now that your schemes will not come to fruition. I refuse to allow anyone to blackmail me or force me into a situation not of my choosing. If compromise is your aim, know that no force in the world can compel me to extend an offer of marriage to anyone *not of my choosing. Should you wish to risk your reputation, the consequences will rest solely upon your head.*

If you mean to curry friendship with my dear sister hoping she will forward your cause, once again you mistake the matter. Miss Darcy is not one to be bought. She has encountered such machinations before and risen above them; she is not so easily deceived by false friendships. Had she not told me of her sorrows only yesterday, I would have consigned your letter to the fire rather than granting you any consequence by way of reply.

Let me disabuse you, madam, of any further notions surrounding an acquaintance with the Darcys of Pemberley. Neither I nor my sister will acknowledge you. Your methods might have found more understanding or fruitful ground had you not openly displayed your duplicitousness. First, you falsely claim that your relations have leased my home and address this missive to my solicitor in London; yet it somehow arrives at my doorstep. Then, you reveal your lack of sense by dating your letter incorrectly—July 5, 1812? What madness is this? I assure you, madam, that it is the year 1810 and has been so since the first of January.

You did not even bother to determine that my railing is blue, not green, with no tracks adorning the stoop. Nor did you observe that my parlour window is completely intact.

I will write to Farnsworth-Durham immediately, informing them of your despicable efforts and warning them to consign any letters from you to the fire. I will not be put upon by an upstart; if your name carried any weight, surely it would be familiar to me.

I shall waste no further words on you, madam. Cease your paltry efforts at once.

Yours, etc.,

Fitzwilliam Darcy

He signed his name with a flourish and reread the missive. His tone in the letter was hard and unyielding, precisely as he intended. The interloper who received it deserved nothing less; he reserved compliments and pleasantries for proper friends.

Pleased with his work, he sanded and sealed the letter, pressing his signet ring into the hot wax. He stood and walked to the entrance hall, placing the letter atop the outgoing post. Miss Elizabeth Bennet would not bother him any longer.

Darcy straightened his coat. Smythe appeared with his hat and gloves. "Thank you," Darcy said, donning the hat. "Is the carriage ready?"

"It is, sir," Smythe replied. His faithful butler opened the door, and Darcy walked out into the warm sunlight. He boarded the carriage, and the footman closed the door with a soft snick.

Leaning back against the squabs, Darcy pulled out a small notebook and examined his list. As he read, a niggling sense of guilt came over him. Perhaps his reply to Miss Bennet was a *touch* too harsh. It was of no matter, though. What was done was done, and he would leave the unknown miss in no doubt of his sentiments. Georgiana would be safe from at least this false friendship and would have nothing to worry about.

The carriage drew up before the bookshop, and Darcy alighted. Pushing the lingering guilt away, he entered, determined to find the perfect novel for his sister's upcoming birthday.

Chapter Two

July 1812
Lake House
Ramsgate
Elizabeth

Miss Elizabeth Bennet, lately of Longbourn in Hertfordshire, blinked against the bright sunlight streaming into her bedchamber. Confusion reigned for a moment before she recalled she was no longer in her familiar childhood room, but in the luxurious bedchamber of the house her brother-in-law had leased in Ramsgate. Mr Charles Bingley had married Elizabeth's elder sister Jane just six months ago. The pair were blissfully happy, though Jane's delicate condition had brought on constant nausea and fatigue, prompting her husband to seek a house near the sea for the duration of her confinement.

Jane had begged Elizabeth to accompany them when they left Netherfield Park a week ago. "I cannot do without you, you know," she said from her bed when her younger sister had visited her one afternoon. Elizabeth recalled Jane's pallid complexion and her wan features as she presented her offer. Even if Jane had looked half as miserable as she most certainly was, Elizabeth knew she could never have refused her sister's request.

"You may rest easy, dearest," Elizabeth said that afternoon. "I am certain my father can spare me; it will leave only our three younger sisters at home, but he has suffered through such before."

Jane expressed her gratitude fervently, reaching out to clasp Elizabeth's hand. "Thank you. It will ease my mind to know that my household will not suffer neglect because of my lack of health."

"If Aunt Gardiner is to be believed, your illness will not be of long duration. She says the sickness usually subsides after a few months."

Jane let out a soft snort. "The last few weeks have been trying enough. I can scarcely imagine how I will survive for several more *months*!"

"Will you be able to endure a carriage ride?" Elizabeth was deeply concerned for Jane; never had she seen her sister look so ill. "Will the rocking and swaying not exacerbate your condition?"

Jane's face turned a sickly shade of green, and Elizabeth promptly held a bowl under her chin. Jane heaved, though the nausea had long since relieved her of her breakfast. She sat back and used a handkerchief to wipe her lips.

"Mr Jones insists that the sea air will help me," she said, closing her eyes and leaning into her pillow. "Charles's physician agrees, and since my husband will not be dissuaded, to the sea we shall go."

"Have you a location in mind?"

"We have had a letter in reply to our inquiries. There is a house in Ramsgate that has recently come available to lease. Charles will take it for the year. That will give time for the babe to be born and for the little one to grow strong enough to travel home."

Elizabeth had never been to the sea, and the mention of Ramsgate sent a thrill of excitement through her. "Will you tell me of it?" She blushed a little as she detected the eager pleading in her voice.

Jane smiled serenely. "If the description holds true, it is a handsome house. The residence is in a fashionable location and only minutes from the seaside. Lake House—that is its name—has four family chambers and three guest chambers. At the back of the house lies a pleasing garden, enclosed on three sides by a tall brick wall, offering a sense of privacy while leaving the fourth side open to the sea. The public rooms include a music room, a parlour, a sitting room, dining room, and more."

"It sounds like a delightful prospect. Is there a lake nearby?"

Jane looked puzzled. "Why do you ask? Is the sea not enough for you?"

Elizabeth swatted her sister playfully and laughed. "I only wonder at the name *Lake House*. What a peculiar name if the structure is not anywhere near a lake!"

"What a silly thing to quibble about!" Jane laughed, as Elizabeth had intended her to. "I am unsure whence the name comes, but I am certain that there is a logical explanation."

"When are we to depart?"

Jane's eyes drifted closed, and she yawned. "Charles would like to leave immediately. I have convinced him to delay for three days. That will give you enough time to ready yourself, and for my dear husband to approach Papa about stealing you away from him."

"Then I shall leave you now," Elizabeth replied, wiping a stray lock of hair from Jane's forehead. "The sooner I pack my trunks, the happier my brother will be!"

"Have him escort you back to Longbourn. He can speak to Papa."

Elizabeth nodded and stood. She bent and kissed Jane's forehead and quietly left the room.

That was ten days past. After securing her father's reluctant consent, Elizabeth had made ready to depart immediately. Her haste pleased her brother, and the little party left Netherfield only two days after Jane had issued her invitation. Their journey had been slow, with frequent stops to ensure Jane's comfort, but now they had arrived at Lake House and Elizabeth held high hopes that her sister's condition would soon improve.

Rising from her bed, she rang for a maid, eager to begin her day. Jane had instructed the housekeeper, Mrs Palmer, to speak to Elizabeth on household matters, and Charles had requested that Elizabeth take an inventory of the house and its conditions to forward on to the solicitor. She had promptly completed the task and left the letter on the salver the previous day to be posted. She smiled as she recalled the green tracks on the front stoop, which were no doubt left by a mischievous cat when the groundskeeper painted the railing. Overall, the house was in good order, leaving Elizabeth with little to report in her letter to the solicitor.

The maid assigned to her entered her chamber. She was slight of stature, with corn-yellow hair and rosy cheeks. "Good morning, Susan," Elizabeth greeted her, and the maid dipped a curtsey in response.

"I believe the blue gown will suit today," she said, gesturing to the ensemble she had already selected. In a trice, the gown was on, and Susan had fastened the buttons. Elizabeth sat before the mirror, watching as the maid worked miracles on her unruly locks, twisting and pulling them into some semblance of order.

"I am impressed," she told the maid. "I have never seen one so adept at handling my wild curls!"

"I have had much practise, madam," Susan replied demurely. "There are several girls here with hair like yours. They let me at their locks occasionally."

"Time well spent, to be sure," Elizabeth murmured. "Thank you. I shall be off to break my fast now. Has Mrs Bingley awakened?"

Susan shook her head. "No, madam. Mr Bingley requested no one disturb her until she rings for a maid."

"Very well, then. I would be foolish not to heed my dear brother's wishes. Thank you again." Rising from her seat, she left the room, pausing briefly to recall the way to the dining room. She soon remembered the correct door and joined her brother there.

"Good morning, Lizzy," Charles said from his place at the table. "How do you do today? Are you rested after our long journey?"

"I am well enough," she replied. "What a fine spread! Rashers of bacon, scones, eggs, honey ham, and fresh fruit. I must say, I feel quite spoiled!"

"The staff are eager to please. From what I have gathered, the house has been empty for some time."

Elizabeth's brow furrowed. "Was it not let to another before now?"

Charles shook his head but did not look up from his plate. "It is a family residence. I do not know why it has been vacant for so long, and I did not think to enquire, but as it is well-maintained, I have no grounds for complaint."

She shrugged and took her seat at Charles's left. Once she filled her plate with her favourites, she put a generous helping of fruit preserves on her scone and took a bite. It tasted every bit as heavenly as it smelled, and she sighed in pleasure.

"Have you anything in particular you would like me to accomplish today?" she asked her brother-in-law.

Charles looked up from his plate. "You are not here to be a servant, Lizzy," he chided teasingly.

Elizabeth rolled her eyes. "I know. But I am here to help Jane and to make things easier for her."

"I imagine you ought to consult with her on her expectations." Charles dabbed his lips with his serviette. "Neither of us wishes you to work yourself to the bone whilst you are our guest. Take time to see the ocean and visit the shops. Jane will likely request only that you seek her approval of menus and any large decisions that need to be made. If you can relieve her of the minutiae that does not require her personal attention, that would be ideal."

Elizabeth nodded and took another bite of her scone. "I will wait until she awakens and then have a discussion with her. I imagine she will be abed for some time. She looked exhausted when we arrived yesterday."

A look of concern flashed across Charles's face before his customary smile blossomed. "Jane will be well. It is only a matter of time."

Elizabeth nodded and wondered who he was trying to convince. Of course, Jane would be well! Women had come through pregnancy since the beginning of time, and her dear sister would be no different.

Once he finished his meal, Charles stood. "I shall be in the study if you have need of me," he said. "There are a few matters of business I need to attend to. Did you know there was already a letter from Netherfield's steward waiting for me when we arrived?"

Elizabeth chuckled. "Such is the lot of a landowner. Will you purchase the estate, do you think?"

Her brother shrugged. "It is as good as an estate as any, I suppose. I once considered purchasing farther north, but…" He shook his head. "No matter. I can consider my options this autumn when it comes time to renew the lease."

"Very prudent," Elizabeth agreed. "I shall check in on Jane when I am done here."

Her brother nodded and left the room, leaving Elizabeth to finish her meal in solitude.

Jane was awake when Elizabeth entered her sister's chamber a half-hour later. She was propped up in bed, her face a pasty white. A flaxen braid cascaded over one shoulder. Had she not looked so dreadfully ill, Elizabeth thought Jane would have presented a charming picture.

"Good morning, Jane dear," she said softly. "Are you feeling any better?"

"I feel rather dreadful." Jane's voice sounded raspy, doubtless from losing the contents of her stomach so many times. "I have such nervous flutterings and my head aches and... Oh! Am I turning into Mama, Lizzy?"

Elizabeth wanted to laugh at Jane's panicked expression but instantly sought to reassure her sister. "Oh, Jane! You are far too serene to become like our mother. Now, have you attempted to eat anything this morning? I can ring for some toast and ginger tea."

"That sounds lovely. I hope I can keep it down. Nothing seems to agree with me."

"I planned to consult with the housekeeper this morning on the menu for the week," Elizabeth continued. "Do you have any particular requests?"

"Since I very much doubt that I will join you at the dinner table, I leave everything up to you. You might ask Charles for his preferences. However, if there are any decisions you feel unequal to making without my aid, I will step in, but the management of the house is yours, if you have no objections."

Elizabeth smiled and patted her sister's hand. "Very well. I will ring for your toast and tea and then go to meet Mrs Palmer." She stood and pulled the bell.

Jane nodded weakly and Elizabeth turned to leave the room. She met her sister's maid, Sally, just outside the bedchamber door. "Mrs Bingley wishes for toast and ginger tea," she directed the maid, pleased with her expeditious appearance.

Sally curtseyed and departed immediately, leaving Elizabeth to make her way downstairs to Mrs Palmer's office.

Elizabeth had the menus sorted forty-five minutes later, and then retired to the sitting room with a book. So absorbed was she that she startled when the butler knocked upon the door.

"The post has arrived, Miss Bennet," he announced sombrely, holding out the salver.

"Thank you, Smythe," she replied, taking the stack of letters. There were only three, two of which were addressed to her brother. The third displayed her name in a bold, masculine hand, and Elizabeth's brow furrowed in confusion. She flipped the letter over to read the return direction, and her jaw dropped open in shock.

"*The Lake House?*" she breathed, her voice barely a whisper. She set aside her brother's letters and quickly tore the seal on her own. Impatiently, she began to read. With each word, her anger grew. Her cheeks flushed as she scowled.

"How *dare* he!" she hissed under her breath. "Who does this man think he is to berate me so? *I* lack wit? What sort of trickery is this—to imply the house is not under lease and that the year is only 1810?" She stood, intent on informing her brother of the mysterious letter at once. She was halfway to the door when she paused. Charles had enough to worry about. Jane's health was tenuous, and he was already being inundated with letters from his steward and his business managers.

There was even a letter from his younger sister, Caroline Bingley, no doubt asking for an advance on her allowance. No, Elizabeth would handle this matter herself.

"Whoever this Mr Fitzwilliam Darcy is, he has met his match." She strode over to the writing desk and pulled a clean sheet of paper towards her.

> *Lake House*
> *Ramsgate*
> *July 6, 1812*
>
> *Dear Mr Darcy,*
> *I am unaccustomed to being so maligned, whether in person or in letter form, and so take this opportunity to address the accusations laid at my door, unfair as they are. You are as unknown to me as I am to you, and I can only rejoice that it is so. I am uncertain how you acquired a letter that was clearly addressed to another, and more baffled still that you opened it.*
> *It will bruise your ego, to be sure, to know that I have never heard of the Darcys of Pemberley, and so it is perfectly clear that your name carries as little weight as my own. You might as well be the Prince of Persia for all I care. If you are a gentleman—and I have my doubts as to such—I can only conclude that your education was sadly lacking as to the proper behaviour of one bearing that title. How dare you question my integrity and claim that I have breached propriety, hoping to gain admittance into your circles!*
> *I know nothing of your sister, either, and can only pity her for having such an officious and proud elder brother! I assure you, sir, that nothing in the world could convince me to marry a man who so blatantly seeks to*

wound another, casting aspersions and making accusations with nary a thought to the facts.

I will inform you that the railing of Lake House is indeed green, and had I a way to capture it, I would enclose the evidence in this letter immediately. The year is 1812, and I shall drop a nugget of information in your lap to prove it. In the year 1810, Napoleon annexed the Kingdom of Holland as the first part of the French Empire. The official annexation was on the ninth of July. I am certain it will be some time before you receive confirmation of my claim, should you choose to send out inquiries. The Little Corsican's reign of terror is just beginning, and the war will claim many lives in the years to follow. Lest you accuse me of being a French spy, I will tell you I read of the event myself in the London paper when it arrived at my father's estate.

Your sister has my pity for having to face such false friends. With all my heart, I sincerely hope that Miss Darcy will find a loyal companion, one who esteems her for herself and not for any other reason. I do wonder whether her 'friends' would be so interested in you had they been the recipient of letters such as the one I received this morning.

My reputation is safe from you or from any other gentleman, and I assure you that my brother-in-law is more than capable of protecting me from one such as yourself.

If Farnsworth-Durham deigns to acknowledge your orders, I should be surprised. It is their establishment that brokered the lease of the house to my brother, after all.

I bid you to have the day you deserve, sir, and beg you to importune me no further with your petty accusations.

Yours, etc.,

Elizabeth Bennet

She signed her name with relish and examined her work carefully. It was bewildering how her letter had ended up in the hands of this

Fitzwilliam Darcy. The house had stood empty for a long time; perhaps some interloper was hiding in the attic?

She shook her head and chuckled. How very gothic it all sounded! Papa would scold her for being as silly as Lydia.

She sanded the paper and folded the letter carefully. After sealing it, she hesitated, wondering how to address the missive.

He claims he is in residence here. Let him prove it. She scrawled the direction quickly: *To Mr Fitzwilliam Darcy, Lake House, Ramsgate.* With her anger replaced by smugness, Elizabeth left the room and deposited the letter on the salver in the entryway to be posted. Now, only time would reveal the truth.

Chapter Three

July 9, 1810
The Lake House
Ramsgate
Darcy

Darcy rolled his shoulders and leaned back in his chair, his neck aching from hours of poring over the many letters demanding his attention. It seemed the work of a landowner was never done, even when one was on holiday at the seaside.

Mr Hobbs, his steward, wrote of a minor tenant dispute, seeking Darcy's approval for how he had handled the matter. Hobbs, of course, had dealt with it exactly as Darcy would have, a testament to the steward's intelligence and his knowledge of his master's ways. Though he appreciated his faithful servant's efforts to keep him informed, Darcy sometimes wished a few weeks could pass without receiving a letter from him.

Amongst his correspondence was a missive from his friend, Charles Bingley. Charles was younger than Darcy by several years, but their bond was no less for the age difference. Darcy had met Bingley at Gentleman Jack's one afternoon. The wiry young man had drawn a large crowd as he sparred with some of London's best pugilists. Despite his lean physique and light figure, Bingley had beaten his opponents again and again. With each bout, the bets placed grew greater until someone declared they would grant five hundred pounds to the man who could beat Charles Bingley.

The money held no allure, but the young interloper's presence threatened Darcy's undefeated status in the club. He accepted the challenge and stepped into the ring. Tensions were high as the spectators placed new bets. With neither man vanquished yet, no one could be certain how this bout would end.

It took a matter of minutes for Darcy to analyse Bingley's fighting style and to identify his weakness. His left side was slightly weaker than his right, though not by much. A knee injury, perhaps? Unwilling to land a devastating blow to the man's pride, he kept the bout going for some time before striking. Once Darcy went on the offensive, it took only minutes for Bingley to yield.

The spectators cheered wildly, and Darcy collected the five-hundred-pound marker from Viscount Trent, a reckless young man with more money than he knew what to do with. After accepting the onlookers' congratulations, Darcy turned to his opponent, expecting to see dejection and bitterness. Instead, Charles Bingley was grinning widely as he extended his hand.

"Good show!" he cried. "It has been many a year since I faced such a challenge. I do hope we can spar again!"

Perplexed, Darcy replied, "It would be my pleasure. I frequent Gentleman Jack's twice a week."

"Charles Bingley, at your service," the cheerful gentleman said. "Lately of Scarborough, but now dwelling in London."

"Fitzwilliam Darcy," he returned. "Of London and Pemberley."

"Pemberley? Where is that?"

Had Bingley's expression not been so open and honest, Darcy might have thought the man was being disingenuous. "Pemberley is in Derbyshire," he replied.

"Alas, I have never visited that county! Is it as rugged as people say?"

Darcy smiled at Bingley's innocent inquiry. "It is, but I have a long-held fondness for it, nonetheless. Derbyshire is the best of counties, and none can convince me otherwise."

"Come with me to Boodle's and we can speak more of it. I would wish an acquaintance with you if only to have an adequate sparring partner." Bingley grinned and patted his face with a cloth to remove the beads of sweat from his brow.

Darcy nodded. "The idea has merit. I, too, have lacked any real challenge since my cousin left with his regiment."

"Glad to be of service, then. Come now, my treat."

Darcy followed Bingley from the room and soon they were aboard a carriage, trundling off towards Boodle's. They settled into a private parlour and ordered a meal. At first, Bingley's constant flow of conversation was burdensome for Darcy, but he soon realised his new acquaintance required neither loquacity nor detailed responses. Since Bingley spoke more than enough for both, Darcy soon felt himself relaxing and enjoying himself.

Ever cautious, however, he remained alert for any usual signs of social climbing or opportunism that often marked new acquaintances. Bingley exhibited none of these indicators, much to Darcy's relief, and when the man mentioned his two unmarried sisters at another lunch, he was quick to reassure Darcy that he was not one to use his friendships to secure matches for his relations. In consequence, Darcy asked about the Bingley ladies—inquiring about sisters was something he would never dare to do with most gentlemen.

"Louisa is the elder," Bingley said. "She is petite, with brown hair and brown eyes. My sister has been out for two years and is growing fretful that her dowry has yet to attract any suitors. I have told her that her fortune only *just* lessens the stench of its origin, but she refuses to believe me."

Darcy's nose twitched slightly before he schooled his expression. "You are from trade?" he asked.

"Yes. My father made his fortune in the mills and shipping, and though I still hold some interest in the companies, I have sold off most of it. His fondest wish was that I purchase an estate. I have yet to do so." Bingley noted Darcy's look and raised his eyebrows. "Does my background bother you, Darcy?" His cheerful expression had faded, and he regarded Darcy with a shrewd expression. "I wager you never suspected it. I present myself well, and had I not disclosed that detail, I doubt you would have known. I do not shy away from my origins. My father worked hard for what I now enjoy, and I will not be ashamed of it."

Darcy felt a little chagrined at Bingley's words and he swallowed. "I was raised to avoid trade and those associated with it," he confessed. "Though your disclosure has given me pause, I value honesty, and believe trust is necessary in a friendship. Your candour reveals you as forthright and honest, and I will not forfeit a potential acquaintance for such a paltry reason as an accident of birth."

Bingley grinned and raised his glass. "I am pleased to hear you speak so reasonably. Now, where was I? Oh yes, Louisa! She has recently attracted the attention of a gentleman by the name of Reginald Hurst. He is the heir to a decent estate, and my inquiries reveal his father has cut off his allowance due to dissolute living. He seeks a wealthy bride to fund his lifestyle until he inherits. I have tried to dissuade my sister, but she will not listen. She is of age, so if Louisa chooses Mr Hurst, I shall grant her my blessing and release her dowry."

"It is hard watching those we love make poor decisions, especially when they have lifelong consequences."

"Indeed! My sister Caroline is as headstrong as they come. She will be out this season, and I pray she makes a match soon. She does not listen to reason, and I fear she will run roughshod over me. I dislike confrontation and she takes full advantage of that. Have you any sisters, Darcy? Or brothers? I should have liked to have a brother."

"I have one sister. Her name is Georgiana. She is very young, only thirteen, and as sweet and angelic as they come."

"She sounds lovely. Do you have the care for her, or..." Bingley trailed off and waited for Darcy to answer.

"My father died two years ago, and my mother three years before that," he said soberly. "I have had the care of Georgiana since she was eleven. My cousin shares guardianship with me, but his career in the army keeps him from us far too often."

Bingley nodded sympathetically. "Such is the nature of service to our King." Darcy tipped his head in agreement.

Bingley became a frequent visitor to Darcy House, and his easy manner fostered their growing friendship. By summer, Darcy had extended an invitation for him and his sisters to visit Pemberley. He thought he was prepared for their stay, but soon realised he was sorely mistaken. Miss Bingley was by now engaged to Mr Hurst, but Miss Caroline took one look at Darcy and his estate and became unbearable. The avarice that glinted in her eyes was obvious to those who cared to see it, and Darcy found he had to employ certain measures to keep from being left alone with her.

His friendship with Bingley was worth enduring Miss Caroline's presence on occasion.

Darcy shook himself from his musings and opened his friend's letter. As usual, Bingley filled his letter with crossed out words and ink blotches, making it difficult to decipher. The gist of it, though, was that Bingley wished to meet Darcy in London in the autumn. His brother-in-law had requested the use of Bingley's townhouse, and his friend wished to know if he was welcome at Darcy House, if he needed to make an escape.

Darcy penned his reply and added the finished missive to the stack of outgoing mail. He stood and stretched, arching his back against the dull ache that had begun there. *Enough work for today,* he told himself. Georgiana would certainly be waiting for him in the parlour. His shopping expedition had proven fruitful, and he was prepared for his sister's birthday, which was just days away.

He gathered the letters that needed to be posted and left his study to deposit them on the salver. As he moved to place the stack on the shining silver tray, he hesitated. There was a letter there. *Odd.* Smythe had already delivered the post for the day. He scooped it up, slipped it into his pocket to read later, and deposited the stack in his hand onto the salver.

His sister was indeed waiting for him in the parlour. They partook of a delightful tea before taking a walk on the beach. Georgiana's responses pleased Darcy when he quizzed her on her schoolwork. Clearly, she was being attentive to her studies, just as a Darcy should.

Upon returning to the Lake House, Darcy left to dress for dinner. He removed his tailcoat and handed it off to his valet, Williams, fiddling with his cravat in the mirror.

"Sir?" Williams returned, a missive in his hand. "This was in the pocket of your coat. Would you care for it now, or shall I deposit it on your desk?"

The letter. He had forgotten. "I will take it, Williams," he replied, holding out his hand. The valet handed the letter to his master, and Darcy clenched his jaw when he recognised the handwriting. He flipped it over and sure enough, the sender was none other than the presumptuous Elizabeth Bennet.

How dare she! Darcy seethed; he wanted to crumple the letter in his hand. Instead, he allowed Williams to put on his evening coat before sitting down to open it. He broke the seal and unfolded the paper, reading the words. He felt his temper rising, and he tugged at his cravat in irritation, pulling it askew.

Her insults were harsh, and his ego hurt from the notion that this nobody proclaimed him to be of equally inferior status. How had she not heard of the Darcys of Pemberley? Had she been living in a cave or under a rock? And what of her audacious claim that the railing was green? He stood and paced the room; the letter clenched in one hand. Pausing before the window, he looked out at the garden. The flowers were in full bloom, and he allowed their beauty to calm him.

Darcy looked at the missive in his hand and read it once more, pausing on the paragraph about his railing. What was this? Miss Bennet claimed to know the future!

The year is 1812, and I drop a nugget of information in your lap to prove it. In the year 1810, Napoleon annexed the Kingdom of Holland as the first part of the French Empire. The official annexation was on July ninth, and I am certain it will be some time before you receive the information. The Little Corsican's reign of terror is just beginning, and the war will claim many lives in the years to follow. Lest you accuse me of being a French spy, I will tell you I read of the event myself in the London paper when it arrived at my father's estate.

He drew in a sharp breath. Could it be? Everyone was aware of Napoleon's rise to power in France, but would he seek to conquer all of Europe, as Miss Bennet implied? There was only one way to find out. He glanced at the clock; there was still time before dinner to pen a few missives. In the past, he used certain avenues to track his cousin's whereabouts when news was scarce. He would write to his contacts in London. Perhaps they had heard something. But first, these insults could not go unanswered. Something compelled him to put pen to paper, even though he knew there was no need to reply to Miss Bennet's latest letter. Darcy stalked to his desk and sat hard in his chair. He pulled a fresh sheet towards him and dipped his quill into the ink and weighed his words before beginning to write.

The Lake House
Ramsgate
July 9, 1810

To Miss Elizabeth Bennet,
It seems, madam, that my previous correspondence did little to dissuade you from presuming upon my acquaintance, and so I find myself compelled to write again. I am as pleased as you are that we are unknown to each other, for I would hesitate to have the acquaintance of one who possesses such impertinence. Did your mother not teach you to behave better?
How dare you impugn my honour as a gentleman! You claim to have never heard of the Darcys of Pemberley. If you speak the truth, you are not the lady you claim to be, or you are a lowly gentleman's daughter of little means. Nothing else would prevent you from having the information.

You will kindly refrain from writing of my sister. I wrote what I did to protect her, and you will not use her name or her existence to malign me any further.

As for your suppositions that you know the future, by tomorrow, an express will be in London with my contacts there. I expect to have your claims fully refuted. Should they not be… what I shall do then remains to be seen.

I bid you good day and goodbye. Do not contact me and mine again.

Fitzwilliam Darcy

The next day, Darcy found himself unable to focus on his work. The letter from Miss Bennet and his hasty reply consumed his thoughts, and he found that the anger he had felt the night before had softened into curiosity. More importantly, the information she relayed about Napoleon was concerning. Richard Fitzwilliam, his cousin, had just received a promotion to the rank of colonel and granted command of his own unit. If Napoleon were indeed making his way through Europe, it was only a matter of time before Richard found himself in the thick of battle. Darcy's aunt, the Countess of Matlock, would not be pleased.

A noise from the front of the house drew him from his musings, prompting him to leave his study and make his way to the entrance hall. When he opened the front door, shock coursed through him as he saw that someone had painted his formerly blue railing a fashionable green. A servant he recognised as the groundskeeper for the Lake

House yelled at the back of a departing feline, shaking his fist and scolding the beast.

"Kerr! What goes on here?" Darcy asked brusquely.

The groundskeeper straightened and doffed his hat, bowing to his master. "Beggin' yer pardon, sir," he stammered. "A cat ran through the paint and left tracks everywhere. Ah can try tae wipe it up, but ah dinnae ken if it'll work, sir."

"When did I approve this change?" Darcy's tone was curious, not harsh, for he did not remember making this decision, and he was seldom stern with his servants unless absolutely necessary.

"It were last winter, sir," the servant replied. "Mr Smythe made me wait 'til summer tae do the work; what wi' the storms blowin' through since spring. Ah'm finally getting 'roond tae it."

Darcy nodded, and a memory slowly surfaced. He remembered writing to Smythe of the matter in December. All the London homes were utilising the fashionable green, and he had wished for the Lake House to follow suit. Darcy House had already adopted the change. It seems Miss Bennet had been correct... about the railing *and* the tracks made by the cat.

"C-carry on," he stammered slightly. He turned and went back into the house, closing the door behind him. Darcy made his way to his study and collapsed into a chair. He ran his hand over his eyes and stared blankly at the wall. It was simply not possible... was it? Somehow, Miss Bennet was writing to him from the future. When he received the replies to his inquiries, he would know for sure.

Chapter Four

July 15, 1812
The Lake House
Ramsgate
Elizabeth

Elizabeth's days in Ramsgate soon fell into a predictable pattern. After rising each morning, she broke her fast with Charles before looking in on Jane. After insuring her sister's well-being and seeing that she received a tray, Elizabeth would meet with Mrs Palmer to review the menus and any other items that needed her oversight. Since the Bingleys were not entertaining at the moment, meals were simple fare.

Elizabeth quickly endeared herself to the staff. Mr Smythe, the butler, displayed the stoic and serious manner of butlers everywhere, though his eyes twinkled mysteriously more often than not. Elizabeth made it her goal to see the man smile, though her efforts had done nothing more than cause his lips to twitch thus far. Mrs Palmer, a professional and capable member of the household staff, ran Lake House with efficiency, leaving very few matters requiring the mistress's attention on a day-to-day basis.

Besides the pair that the Bingleys had brought with them, they also employed two additional footmen. James and John were six feet tall and burly, much to Charles's delight. The pair were rather singular—a set of twins with nearly identical features. Elizabeth could not tell them apart, but for the scar John had above his left eyebrow.

Lake House also employed Susan, Elizabeth's ladies maid, who was competent and diligent in her duties. Along with Susan, Molly and Martha attended tasks on the upper floors of the house, whilst three additional girls and a lad aided Cook on the lower floors. Lake House had not employed a cook in several years, so Mrs Moore, Netherfield's own mistress of the kitchen, had come with the Bingleys to Ramsgate.

After meeting with Mrs Palmer, a footman would accompany Elizabeth on a walk. She was intent on exploring Ramsgate and wandered as far as she could on foot each day. Her favourite place was the beach, and she found joy in standing and watching the waves as they crashed upon the shore.

After her walk, Elizabeth saw to her correspondence and then partook of a light luncheon. She often joined Jane in her chamber and ate her meals there. However, her sister did little more than pick at the offerings put before her, causing Elizabeth's concern for Jane's welfare to grow. She spent afternoons engaged in solitary pursuits whilst Jane continued to rest. Sometimes Charles offered to squire Elizabeth about the town so she could run her personal errands or visit a sight or two, but business concerns usually occupied him if he was not spending time with Jane.

Her existence was not lonely, but neither was Elizabeth content with how her days progressed. As Jane's cheeks became more and more hollow and she slept longer each day, Elizabeth feared for her sister's life. In desperation, she penned a letter to her Aunt Gardiner, begging for advice on how to best help Jane and improve her sister's health, and was thus engaged when Smythe brought the post to her.

Another letter from the mysterious Mr Darcy had arrived on the tenth, and Elizabeth had almost consigned it to the fire after reading it. The man's officious and pretentious behaviour was difficult to stomach, so she did not bother to pen a reply. Instead, the letter joined the first in the bottom of her trunk.

There were many letters in the post that day, and Elizabeth took the bundle, thanking Smythe warmly. His eyes twinkled as he bowed before departing, and she turned her attention to the small stack of missives in her hand. She set aside two for Charles. The next was for Jane, and Elizabeth was quick to recognise their mama's handwriting. Another was from Papa, making Elizabeth smile—he must be desperate for sensible conversation if he had taken the time to write to his second daughter.

The last letter in the stack caused her to tense, anger rising within her. By now, she was familiar with Mr Darcy's handwriting, having perused his previous correspondence numerous times since receiving them, despite having at first consigned it to her trunk. She turned this new letter over and noted that the return direction remained at *The Lake House*. She marvelled at Mr Darcy's use of the word '*the*' before Lake House. The plaque by the front door simply said '*Lake House*,' and so that was what Elizabeth had called it. Yet, the servants used the same name as Mr Darcy when they spoke of the residence. She briefly wondered if he was the mysterious absent master.

There is no doubt this missive contains more vitriol, she mused. How had this Mr Darcy managed to once again sneak his letter into the stack of post by the front door? It made no sense. Surely, the servants would have noticed an intruder by now.

Carefully, she broke the seal on the back of the missive and unfolded the paper. Taking a deep breath, she began to read.

July 14, 1810

Dear Miss Bennet,

I find myself in a state of uncertainty. Such a predicament has rarely been mine to experience, and I am not certain I enjoy feeling so discomposed. I know not where to begin, and I pray that when I have concluded this missive, you do not think me mad or worse.

First, I must convey my deepest and most sincere apologies for my first two letters. Had I behaved in a more gentleman-like manner, perhaps this letter would be easier to compose. I beg you to forgive my pique and my intemperate words and allow me to begin anew.

My name is Fitzwilliam Darcy, and I am the master of the Lake House. I came by the property through my paternal grandmother, Amelia Lake, who brought this seaside residence as part of her dowry upon her marriage to Gregor Darcy. Lake House soon became *the* Lake House to all who have enjoyed the place since that time.

My family has never let the property before, and I can only assume that there is a sound reason for it by the time the year reaches 1812.

Yes, Miss Bennet, now we come to the most complicated part of this situation. Do you recall in your first letter that you spoke of the green tracks that graced the stairs and landing before the front door? I abused your supposition terribly, and I am now heartily ashamed of myself. You see, just a few days ago, after a long winter and wet spring, there was finally a day fine enough for my staff to carry out an order I made six months prior, and they painted the railing green. Whilst one of my men was going about this business, an intrepid feline dashed through the paint, leaving green tracks all over the steps and landing.

You might well imagine that your letter was all that consumed my mind as I witnessed the event—the servant yelling and shaking his fist at the now-green cat. I had forgotten that the railing was to be changed from blue to green, and so to see first-hand the making of the green tracks you spoke of rendered me speechless.

Shortly after penning my second missive, I sent out inquiries to my sources in London, seeking confirmation of your other information. I have yet to receive word from them, so I must wait patiently for news. I am in no doubt of your honesty, and that England will shortly be neck-deep in war with France. This does not bode well for certain of my family members, and I wish I could convince my cousin to sell his commission. Alas, he is as duty bound as I and will never do it.

So, Miss Bennet, we come to the crux of the matter. It would seem that our letters have somehow traversed through time, for from my end, it is the year 1810, and from yours, it appears to be 1812. I know not how this phenomenon has taken place, and as a logical man, I struggle to believe that it has occurred at all. Despite this, I am holding two letters from you, and I know that any news of Napoleon's annexation of the Kingdom of Holland will permanently dispel my disbelief.

Why, then, were we two chosen to experience this marvel? I do not know, and I will eagerly await a reply to this letter to learn your thoughts. Never have I strayed so far from propriety as I do now, but my curiosity and scientific mind cannot let the matter rest.

To give further proof to my claims of being master of the Lake House, I will give you three bits of truth. The first is that in the nursery upstairs, I carved my name into the wall of the wardrobe, much to my grandmother's vexation. It was done with a penknife, which was promptly confiscated and never returned.

You will find the second truth in the garden. My younger sister hid my father's snuffbox there after his death. It is in the hollow tree that stands by one wall in the garden. Miss Darcy does not know that I am aware of her treasure—she wrapped it in an oilskin to prevent damage. I do hope she has not moved it, lest you prove me a liar.

You will find the third and final item of proof in the music room. Two summers ago, my sister would not cease playing her favourite score despite having long since mastered it, so I hid the offending sheets beneath a chair. The fitting of the upholstery allowed me to slide it into a small gap where no one, not even the servants, would find it. I do feel guilty about that... Georgiana bemoaned the loss for a time before realising she had the piece memorised. Thus, my efforts proved unfruitful. The chair you seek is a deep blue with white embroidered flowers.

Happy hunting, Miss Bennet. I look forward to hearing from you, if you deign to reply. I will understand if my boorish behaviour has poisoned you from ever wishing to speak—or rather write—to me again.

Sincerely yours,

Fitzwilliam Darcy

Elizabeth leaned back in her chair, reeling from shock and disbelief. Could it be? No! It was impossible! How gullible did this Mr Darcy think she was? Besides, he may have planted this supposed evidence to give the impression that he was speaking the truth.

Curiosity prevailed, and Elizabeth rose slowly from her chair. She meandered out of the parlour and upstairs, reading the letter again as she ascended. Her footsteps took her to the nursery. Servants had worked diligently to ready the room, cleaning, polishing furniture, arranging linens, and ensuring everything was prepared for the arrival of Jane's child.

She stood in the doorway, her gaze fixed on the wardrobe that graced the centre of one wall. It was a stately thing, its surface unmarred by damage. *Is this the one Mr Darcy spoke of?* Elizabeth crossed the room and tugged open the doors. She started on one side and examined the interior thoroughly. Finding nothing, she moved to the other. Her hands ran down the damage-free walls of the wardrobe, finding nothing. Just as she was about to give up, she froze as the smooth wood beneath her fingers gave way to rough and splintered wood.

Elizabeth pushed the door open further and crouched down. The rough spot was at the back and was not readily visible or accessible. She craned her neck to see, and there it was, just as he said, the jaggedly carved name *Fitzwilliam Darcy*. The carving's obvious age disproved her belief that this evidence was recent. She idly wondered how someone had discovered Mr Darcy's mischief, but then reasoned that a maid had found it and told all.

Intrigued now, Elizabeth perused the letter for the next bit of 'evidence.' The garden, was it? Eschewing a bonnet, gloves, and walking boots, she left the house in her slippers, hurrying through the door to the little green oasis in search of the hollowed tree. There were few trees in the garden to investigate, and naturally, the last one she searched contained the cavity mentioned in the letter. The tree, a weathered hawthorn, had a stone bench placed conveniently beneath the boughs. Elizabeth climbed inelegantly onto the seat and stretched to reach the hole.

"Miss Darcy must be taller than I," she muttered as she stood on her toes so that she could put her hand into the hole. It was not as deep as she feared, and her fingers struck something immediately. Elizabeth closed her outstretched digits around the item and pulled it out. Without taking a seat, she hastily unfolded an oiled cloth to reveal an elaborate snuff box. It was jewel-encrusted, the gemstones forming an elegant 'D' that Elizabeth recognised from Mr Darcy's seal.

She cracked the lid and noted that the box was empty before carefully securing it once more in the cloth and returning it to the tree.

Two out of three, she mused as she descended from the bench. Her pace quickened once she was back on the ground, and she scurried into the house. Her steps slowed as she closed the door, and brushing an errant curl from her eyes, she made her way to the music room.

Once she entered, Elizabeth turned and locked the door. It would not do for a servant to discover her searching the chair for the music, especially if seen in a rather undignified position.

The blue chair stood near the fireplace at the far end of the room. It was quite comfortable, as Elizabeth had discovered when she sat in it a few days earlier. The dark blue fabric was soft, and the cushions were plump and cosy. Elegantly done, the tiny white embroidered flowers covering the upholstery added a touch of whimsy to the piece. The seat of the chair was trimmed with a ruffle, and this was the first place Elizabeth resolved to look. She crouched down and lifted it, running her hand up under the seat and searched around the seam. It took but a moment for her to find a small split in the chair's fabric. Her hand snaked inside and brushed against something that felt like paper.

Grasping the item and pulling it towards her, Elizabeth backed out from her position before the chair and sat up on her knees. Sure enough, in her hand she held a piece of music, a Mozart composition, its edges frayed from frequent use. There were a few pencil marks here and there along the score, but they were so faded that she could not read them.

After standing and smoothing the music, Elizabeth approached the pianoforte and placed the sheets upon the instrument. Settling herself on the bench, she carefully plinked the tune, imagining Miss Darcy playing it repeatedly until her brother had felt compelled to hide it away.

Her hands dropped to her lap, and she reached into her pocket for Mr Darcy's letter.

"Am I dreaming?" she said aloud to the empty room. With her own curiosity as piqued as Mr Darcy's was, she resolved to reply to his missive as soon as may be.

Chapter Five

July 17, 1810
The Lake House
Ramsgate
Darcy

It ought not to bother him that Miss Bennet had yet to reply to his letter. If they existed in the same time, it might take days or even weeks for letters to pass between them. All the same, from the time he had placed the missive to her on the salver, Darcy impatiently awaited the post. He was uncertain how this strange correspondence worked. Neither was he certain how long it took for the letters to appear—either in Miss Bennet's plane of the residence or his own. Still, with bated breath, he awaited Smythe bringing him the post each morning. He disregarded all other missives until he had searched the pile for a reply to his last letter, ignoring the probing looks his butler cast his way at his eagerness.

It was three days after he 'posted' his last offering when Miss Bennet's return correspondence arrived. Darcy eagerly removed himself to his study and broke the seal, his eyes devouring the words within.

July 15, 1812

Dear Mr Darcy,

At your request, I performed the tasks you set before me in your last letter. I must say you carved rather well for a young lad. I am certain your grandmother had a good laugh in the privacy of her chambers after scolding you soundly for abusing her furniture so abominably. The location of your carving was doubtlessly designed to prevent discovery since I had to crawl inside the wardrobe to see it properly in the bottom left corner.

Likewise, I discovered an elegant snuffbox hidden within the hollow of the garden tree. Rubies and diamonds adorn the engraved D on the top of it. I replaced it at once upon examining it; your sister may yet return for it one day. As for the music, it too was located, and I have endeavoured to play the piece with little success. Miss Darcy must possess genuine talent at the pianoforte to have mastered such a score at so tender an age. I confess, I have avoided most of Mozart's more difficult compositions.

I shall continue by remarking that your apology was both pretty and expertly delivered, leaving me no choice but to forgive you—provided you do not treat me so in the future. I do not possess a resentful temperament; when someone sincerely apologises for wrong-doing, I can do naught but accept and forgive.

The future! What a strange thing to contemplate, for am I not there already, at least from your perspective? How do you imagine this curious series of events has occurred? Surely only the most valiant and exalted of humanity receive such blessings, not someone as insignificant as I. Mayhap it is *you* who has secured such favour from on high. Tell me, have you slain any dragons or captured a pirate ship? Or maybe you saved a village from flood or famine? Which is it, sir, so that I might praise you properly?

All jests aside, what are we to do about this situation? I confess, I do not wish to cease our correspondence now that we have reached a tenuous accord. I wish to know about Lake House... or rather, the Lake House, and all its history! I would even condescend to learn something of its owner, if the master of the house does not see my request as too forward. I confess, my curiosity has risen with each exchange of letters, and now it is at its peak.

As a show of good faith, and a demonstration of hope, I will tell you more about myself. My name is Miss Elizabeth Bennet of Longbourn, Hertfordshire. I am the second eldest of five sisters. It is with my elder sister, Jane, and her husband that I am in residence at the Lake House. Jane is in a delicate condition and requested that I assist her during this time as she prepares for the birth of her child. She and her husband also lease an estate near my home called Netherfield Park.

I have three younger sisters. Mary is next in age to me, followed by Catherine, whom we call Kitty, and finally Lydia. I could regale you with tales of their antics, but I shall reserve those stories for a time when you may request them. I would not wish to presume upon our new acquaintance, nor believe you interested in my ramblings.

My mother and father are both living. Mama is, I hesitate to say, a silly woman, prone to nerves and fits of vapours. She has settled some since Jane married, for it means that if Papa dies, we will not be destitute. A distant cousin is the heir to my father's entailed estate, and as I implied above, my father has no sons on whom he can bestow it.

I do not know what else you would wish to know at this time, and so I shall close by posing questions of my own.

First, where is Pemberley? I could discover the answer myself, but it is far easier to request that you tell me.

Second, do you enjoy reading? You mentioned a scientific mind. I, too, love science and reading. My father has indulged me in my interests, much to Mama's dismay. Some might call me a bluestocking, but if wishing to improve one's mind by extensive reading grants me that appellation, I shall wear it proudly.

Third, will you tell me of your family? You have previously mentioned a sister and a cousin. Have you any other relations? I do, but I shall save that for another time.

I do hope this letter finds you in good spirits. A walk to the shops is in my plans for this afternoon.

Sincerely,

Elizabeth Bennet

Darcy grinned and folded the paper, sliding the letter into his desk with the other missives from Miss Bennet. She was a saucy lass, with a delightful sense of humour. The minor revelations she had shared about her family were equally fascinating. Five sisters! Who could imagine such a thing? With nearly twelve years separating him from Georgiana, Darcy had practically grown up an only child. Richard, too, had only his elder brother, the viscount. Even Anne de Bourgh had no brothers or sisters. It was astonishing for him to imagine so many children in one family.

Darcy considered Miss Bennet's situation. She had not been explicit, but one could infer much from her words. With Longbourn entailed away from the female line, the daughters must not have a large dowry—not surprising, considering there were *five* of them—and so Mrs Bennet worried endlessly about providing for her children should her husband die. Miss Bennet's elder sister must have married well, for the matron's worries seemed to have lessened.

Miss Bennet had mentioned her sister's condition. Children were a blessing, and surely Miss Bennet felt excited. Yet, Darcy wondered at the nonchalant tone his new friend used when writing of her sister's expected child. Might there to be cause for concern?

He then turned his thoughts to the three questions Miss Bennet had posed in closing. They were simple enough to answer, and it would be no hardship to satisfy her curiosity.

The door to his study opened, and Darcy looked up, his reverie broken. His sister, Georgiana, peeked in timidly, offering a shy smile.

"Georgiana! Do come in." He beckoned her, and she pushed the door open a little farther, stepping into the room.

"An express has arrived for you," she said softly. "I told Smythe I would deliver it."

"That was kind of you." Darcy's brow wrinkled in concern. "Do you recognise the sender?"

Georgiana shook her head. "The direction is unfamiliar to me." She crossed the room and handed the missive to her brother.

"Thank you," he said, accepting it. "I shall read this and then join you for tea. Afterwards, we might visit the shops."

Georgiana's countenance brightened, and she nodded eagerly.

"Very well. I shall be along shortly." He waved her off, and she bounded out of the room, a stark reminder that despite her maturing figure, Georgiana remained very young.

Darcy broke the seal and scanned the brief letter. It was from London; one of his contacts had written to verify Miss Bennet's offer of proof. The letter ended with a query to know how he had come by the information before even the Foreign Office had received word. Darcy simply shook his head.

"They would not believe me if I told them," he said in amusement. Stowing the letter in his desk drawer beside Miss Bennet's growing pile of correspondence, he rose and made his way to the parlour for tea.

Later that evening, Darcy sipped a glass of port before retiring. Georgiana had long since gone to bed, leaving the house quiet and peaceful. Not that it was anything but quiet and peaceful when she was awake. With only two residents in the fashionable house, it was never noisy or chaotic. What must it be like to dwell in a home filled with joy, laughter, and bustling *people?* Miss Bennet must have enjoyed an enviable childhood. Pemberley was big enough that even twelve brothers and sisters could not have filled its rooms, though they would have certainly added more life to the grand estate.

Unable to calm his mind, Darcy went to the writing desk in his chamber and took up a fresh piece of paper. He would write to Miss Bennet, answering her questions and posing some of his own.

He wrote hastily, without regard for ink blots or proper form, driven by the need to put his thoughts to paper. Once finished, he leaned back and surveyed the mess, a chuckle escaping his lips.

"My old tutor would have taken his switch to my knuckles if he had seen this," he muttered with a soft snicker. Setting the blotted sheet aside, he drew forth a sheet of high-quality paper. This time, he copied the letter with more care, giving the work the attention it deserved. When he finished, he sanded the missive, preparing to fold and seal it. He paused, suddenly struck by thoughts of scientific experiments swirling in his mind.

Could it be possible, he wondered, to transport objects within the letters? If so, what should he send to test it? After a moment of consideration, Darcy then pulled a two-penny piece from the small drawer in the writing desk. He folded the letter, positioning the coin at the seal, and poured the hot wax over it before pressing his seal firmly into the blob. Jotting a few more lines on his letter, he explained the nature of his experiment to Miss Bennet. Satisfied, he addressed the letter, and set it by his bedside, ready to post the next morning. At last, feeling the weight of the day, he slipped beneath the coverlet and drifted into sleep.

He awoke at his customary early hour the next morning, rang for his valet, and dressed with his usual efficiency. Letter in hand, he descended to the entryway where he placed the missive on the salver with the other outgoing post. How long, he wondered, would it take for Miss Bennet to receive his letter? And more curiously, would the coin remain or magically vanish?

Still preoccupied, Darcy entered the dining room, where the servants had breakfast laid out and waiting. Georgiana had yet to come down; she seldom rose before nine o'clock. Alone with his thoughts, Darcy idly pushed his food around the plate. After several minutes, he stood and left the room. Perhaps a walk would clear his mind.

Smythe fetched his hat and gloves upon request, and Darcy set out from the house, walking the short distance to a nearby park. Numerous paths wound through the grounds, and Darcy chose the most secluded, his thoughts consuming him.

I ought not to be so preoccupied with Miss Bennet and this enigma, he chastised himself. There were, after all, many matters demanding his attention. His steward had written once more, and several letters of business awaited his reply. Never before had one of the fairer sex so captivated him, and he had yet to even meet the woman.

What was he thinking? Meet Miss Bennet? How absurd! He knew next to nothing about her. What if she was hideous? What if she bore a mole on her brow or was disfigured? Worse still, what if she was of Caroline Bingley's character? Could a woman be so well-spoken and yet a simpering sycophant? It was entirely possible!

And what of this sister? Miss Bennet had implied that her elder sister had married well. Was it a love match, or had she employed arts and allurements to secure the gentleman's affections?

Furthermore, could Darcy dare to trust the words of a stranger when he could not confirm the truth himself? He paused. Maybe he *could* verify certain details. He knew the name of her estate and its location. Why, he could even surmise the name of her sister's estate. Had not Miss Bennet mentioned Netherfield Park in her first letter and confirmed that it was of that neighbouring estate that her sister was now mistress?

Nodding to himself, Darcy directed his steps back towards the Lake House. It was regrettable, yet necessary, that he had grown so suspicious. Poor Georgiana was now learning the same hard lessons he had once faced in school: trust must be earned, not freely granted. Pledges of good faith were a thing of the past for them both.

When Darcy returned to the house, he found his breakfast more palatable. Georgiana soon entered the breakfast room, sparing him the solitude of eating alone. She rambled on about her history lesson, and though distracted, Darcy replied at all the appropriate moments. When they finished their meal, Georgiana excused herself, citing the need to finish her French before they walked on the beach.

Darcy spent the rest of the morning penning several letters to his contacts in London. Within a week, the Bow Street Runners would have his instructions and begin their enquiries into one Miss Elizabeth Bennet of Longbourn. By the end of the month, he would possess all the particulars and would easily determine whether Miss Bennet had ever offered him anything less than the truth.

Pleased with his efforts and now thoroughly fatigued, Darcy leaned back in his chair and closed his eyes. Perhaps he could rest, if only for a short while, before Georgiana begged to return to the beach.

Chapter Six

July 20, 1812
The Lake House
Ramsgate
Elizabeth

Elizabeth ran a hand over her face and sighed as she leaned against the wall outside of Jane's bedchamber door. Her poor sister... Jane grew more drawn with each passing day and Elizabeth did not know what more she could do to help. Her sister could keep nothing down but a bit of broth and weak ginger tea, and she now slept far more than she was awake. Charles, frantic with worry, had written to his physician in London, begging him to come to Ramsgate to see his wife.

No reply had come from Elizabeth's Aunt Gardiner, either. Mrs Bennet would be of little help; Elizabeth knew her mama had been one of the fortunate women who had never suffered so whilst with child.

Elizabeth pushed away from the wall and made her way downstairs to the music room. The music she had found awaited her, and she spent the next half hour practising the first few bars. The piece was complex, but she was determined to learn it as best she could.

Smythe entered the room a moment later, bearing the post. Elizabeth accepted it, moving away from the instrument and placing it atop the stack of correspondence she had neglected in recent days whilst tending to Jane. A letter from her Aunt Gardiner lay at the top of the pile, and she eagerly broke the seal and began to read.

My dear Lizzy,

I was much aggrieved to receive such distressing news of our sweet Jane! Whilst I have heard of ladies suffering in such a manner, it was never my fate during any of my confinements. Although I endured discomfort in the early months with each of my babes, it always eased before I felt the quickening.

I would urge you summon a physician or midwife to examine your sister. If she can stomach broth and tea, it is some comfort, though not enough. Insist that she drink as much as she is able, and we must pray that her illness subsides soon.

We are all well here in London and look forward to seeing you as soon as may be. Pray, keep me informed as to Jane's condition.

With love,

M. Gardiner

Elizabeth huffed in irritation. Her aunt's letter offered no new advice—they had tried everything. It was vexing and frustrating in every way. Watching Jane waste away was agony, and poor Charles was beside himself. He spent nearly every moment at his wife's side, leaving the room only briefly each day.

After setting the letter aside, Elizabeth sifted through the remaining post. Her eyes landed on the now-familiar handwriting of Fitzwilliam Darcy. Grateful for the distraction, she broke the seal and began to read.

July 17, 1810

Dear Miss Bennet,

I am pleased that you unearthed everything I intended you to find. I had wondered whether any of it remained, or if the staff had cleared it away long ago. Perhaps they had already replaced the blue chair or removed the garden tree.

If my grandmother laughed upon discovering my youthful folly, I know not. What I do recall is her scolding and my confinement to bed for the afternoon, without the reward of any sweets. My father's rebuke followed shortly after, along with a stern lecture on respecting the property of others.

I wonder if my sister has forgotten she placed Father's snuffbox in the tree. I am surprised to learn from your letter that it is still there. Had she remembered its location, surely, she would have retrieved it by now. As for the music, play it if you must; at least I am not present to endure the tune once more!

Georgiana is quite gifted at the pianoforte, her skills growing daily. Whilst I admire her dedication and encourage her pursuit, I must often tempt her away from the keys, as her singular focus on music had led to the neglect of other important tasks.

I am gratified that you found my apology acceptable and grateful for your forgiveness. I will do my utmost to treat you as the lady you are and never again behave in such an ungentlemanlike manner, I assure you.

The future is an intriguing notion. I once imagined it to be rather straightforward, yet now I find myself uncertain. How do our letters transcend time? I cannot say, nor can I fathom where to search for the answer.

You speak of being no one special. It would be dreadfully rude of me to disagree with a lady, but by agreeing, I would once again fall prey to those ungentlemanlike manners I have sworn to eschew. And so, I will simply say that I, too, have no heroics attached to my name, and do not know why I am favoured with this extraordinary experience. I humbly implore you to reserve your praise for one who truly deserves it.

Enormous pleasure fills me with your desire to continue our correspondence. I, too, desire it. The entire situation is intriguing, and it would be a disservice to abandon such a mystery before it reaches a conclusion.

You asked about the Lake House. As mentioned previously, it was named for my paternal grandmother, Amelia Lake. Her father built it for her mother, and it became part of her dowry upon marriage to my grandfather. My family spent many joyful summers within its walls and garden. Grandmama always took great care in maintaining the grounds. As a boy, wandering amongst the blooms felt like exploring a foreign land.

Life in Hertfordshire sounds ideal. As for me, there are only two Darcys left: my sister and myself. Miss Darcy—Georgiana—is much younger, and though she is a dear companion, it would have been a pleasure to have a brother or a sister nearer to my age.

Your father's ability to manage a household with six females intrigues me. My own father, I daresay, would have sought refuge in his study to escape the ensuing cacophony. Then again, Pemberley is vast enough that such noise would not have overwhelmed him so easily.

My Aunt Catherine would have strong words regarding an estate entailed away from the female line. She is quite vocal in her opinions, convinced that a woman—she—is as capable of managing an estate as any man. Her husband did not see fit to enact such an arrangement, though, and upon his passing, left the entirety of his estate, Rosings Park in Kent, to his only child—my cousin, Anne.

Now to your questions: Pemberley is in Derbyshire near the village of Lambton. From the estate, the peaks are visible, and whilst I acknowledge a measure of bias, I declare it is the finest place in the world.

There is much to say about Pemberley but suffice it to mention the more notable features: a lake, a trout stream, a dower house, and both formal and informal gardens. My preference lies with the informal gardens, where nature blends seamlessly with the artistry of human design.

As for favourite books, such a thing is impossible to name—like choosing a single star from the heavens. Pemberley's library is vast, and a testament to the work of many generations. The library at Darcy House holds equal treasure. I imagine you have discovered the modest collection at the Lake House by now. Whilst serious reading is my preference, I also take pleasure in novels, and since Georgiana loves them, I read each one myself before granting her permission to do so.

I have mentioned some of my family in this letter, but as you have requested, here is a more detailed account: Beyond Georgiana and myself, the family includes aunts, uncles, and cousins. My father was an only child, but my mother had one brother and one sister. I already mentioned my Aunt Catherine who resides in Kent with her daughter, Anne. Unfortunately, Anne is sickly, and her mother coddles her excessively. Lady Catherine has long hoped for a match between her daughter and me, but I have been steadfast in my refusal.

My mother's brother is the Earl of Matlock, Uncle Hugh Fitzwilliam, whom I hold in great esteem. We affectionately know his wife, Lady Matilda Matlock, as Aunt Tilda. Their sons are Viscount Arthur Bramwell and the Honourable Colonel Richard Fitzwilliam. Bramwell is older than I, but Richard and I were inseparable as children. Presently, Richard serves in His Majesty's army, and your news of Napoleon has heightened my concern for his safety.

Now, allow me to pose my own inquiries: You mentioned your father's estate is entailed away from the female line. Who stands to inherit it, if not his daughters? I would be interested to hear of any extended relations beyond your immediate family.

How fares your sister? My mother suffered greatly whilst expecting my sister, and I have often been told that it was a miracle she carried her to term.

What pursuits do you enjoy? Riding and hunting are personal favourites, and my estate offers ample opportunity for fishing—a pastime I enjoy when at leisure.

I eagerly anticipate your reply, though it seems there is little predictability in the time one must wait between letters. My impatience has only grown with each passing day.

Sincerely yours,

Fitzwilliam Darcy

Postscript: I have undertaken an experiment and placed a coin beneath the seal of this letter. Should it arrive with the letter, we shall know that objects, besides our words, can traverse the boundaries of time. If it does not, we will learn there are limits to this curious form of communication—and I suspect one of my servants will chance upon the coin somewhere in the house.

"Well, well, Mr Darcy." Elizabeth murmured. "It seems we have a greater connexion than we suspected!" She turned the letter over and examined the wax seal. There, embedded within was a coin. She smiled. It would seem that Mr Darcy's servants would not, after all, find a stray coin in his house. Resolving to answer the letter later that evening, Elizabeth went in search of Charles.

She found her brother in his study, his hair dishevelled as though he had been running his fingers through it repeatedly. His countenance was pale and drawn with anxiety.

"Are you well, Charles?"

"Hardly. It will be days before my physician can come from London, and I have yet to find a suitable doctor or midwife here in Ramsgate to attend my dearest Jane." Charles sighed, his breath shaking as he did. "What will become of her, Lizzy? I cannot lose her." He buried his face in his hands and sobbed.

Elizabeth stepped forward and rested a hand on his shoulder. "You will *not* lose her," she said firmly, infusing her voice with as much confidence as she could muster. "Jane is strong, and with both of us by her side, she will eventually recover. Aunt Gardiner's letter assures me we are doing everything right. It is only a matter of time before the nausea she is experiencing abates."

"I pray you are correct. I cannot bear to imagine what might happen if you were not."

"You will see, brother," Elizabeth replied lightly. "Jane would never be so discourteous as to remain ill too long, especially with houseguests! What would she say if she knew I had refused every invitation delivered to your door?"

Charles's lips twitched, a faint smile breaking through his otherwise worried features. "I am more concerned about what Mama Bennet would say if she knew I was failing in my duty to 'throw you in the path of rich men.'"

She swatted him playfully. "Heaven forfend! Mama would never forgive us! It is settled, then. When Jane is well, we will attend every party and soiree in the hope of finding me a suitor." Elizabeth grinned even as her thoughts wandered to her mysterious friend from the past. *He* was someone she would like to meet.

"Thank you, Lizzy," Charles said, rising to his feet. "I believe I will look in on Jane now. Could you send for more broth and tea?"

"Of course." She patted his shoulder and turned to leave the room.

"Lizzy?"

She turned and regarded him steadily.

"I promise you will see *some* society before leaving Ramsgate. It cannot be easy for you to be confined to the house so much."

She smiled softly. "Your consideration does you credit, but I promise I have nothing to lament. Caring for Jane, and for the house in her stead, is my privilege. I am pleased to do it."

Charles nodded, and Elizabeth left the study to request a tray for Jane. Once it was prepared, she carried it upstairs to her sister's chamber. Her brother sat in the chair that he had placed beside Jane's bed to remain near her, clasping her hand in his own. Jane lay back on the pillow, her face turned towards him with a gentle smile on her lips. They both looked up as Elizabeth entered, and Charles stood to take the tray.

"How do you fare, dear Jane?" Elizabeth asked, perching on the edge of the bed.

"I believe I am a bit better today," Jane murmured. Her voice was still raspy, but there was a hint of colour to her cheeks.

"Then let us attempt to put some of Cook's nourishing broth into you," Elizabeth said. She and Charles helped Jane into a sitting position, placing a few pillows behind her back, and then set the tray across her lap. Elizabeth began to feed her sister but felt a pang of disappointment when, after only half the bowl, Jane turned her head away.

"No more, Lizzy," Jane said. "If I wish to keep it down, I must stop."

Elizabeth shared a glance with Charles but did not protest. She placed the spoon next to the bowl and moved the tray to the side table. "We can try more in a little while," she said, struggling to mask her frustration and worry.

"I kept the broth down at breakfast," Jane said. "That must be a good sign. Do you not think so?"

"I think it is an *excellent* sign," Charles ventured. "Shall I read to you now, my love?"

Jane shook her head. "I wish to rest," she replied. "I know you have work that needs doing. Better yet, take Lizzy to the shops. She has not been out of this house in days!"

"I am content to remain here," Elizabeth protested lightly.

"I insist," Jane said firmly. "Sally is here to look after me."

Ultimately, Elizabeth and Charles left the house at Jane's insistence. Whilst concern for her sister lingered, Elizabeth breathed a sigh of relief upon stepping out into the fresh air.

"It is wonderful that the park is so close, is it not?" she asked Charles. "We need not call for the carriage and we will still be close to the Lake House."

Charles agreed, but gave her a puzzled glance, and together they walked down the lane towards the small green. *I shall have to be cautious of how I refer to the Lake House in front of others*, Elizabeth chided.

They strolled in companionable silence, each lost in their own thoughts. Charles appeared contemplative, though his worry seemed to have eased slightly. Elizabeth's mind drifted to the unanswered letter from Mr Darcy. Various responses fluttered through her thoughts, and she smiled, wondering how he might react to her impertinence.

"Look out!" A shout drew Elizabeth from her reverie, and she looked up just in time to see a massive dog bounding towards her.

Never in her life had she seen such a large animal! The beast must have stood over six feet tall on its hind legs.

Charles quickly pulled her aside, off the walking path, as the huge black dog barrelled past, its lead flying wildly behind it. Just when she thought it would continue on, the animal skidded to a halt and turned to inspect them both.

Elizabeth's brother pulled her farther behind him. "Back!" he commanded, but the creature paid him no heed. The beast sniffed about Charles's pockets, clearly searching for something. "I have nothing for you in there!" Charles said, laughing as he pushed its wet nose away.

"Griswold!" came a shout from further up the lane. "Come back here, boy!"

The dog's ears pricked, and he turned towards the man running up the path. In a few quick steps, the dog turned and went to him, sitting on his haunches and panting as though he had not just led his master on a merry chase.

"Shame on you, Griswold!" the man scolded, scooping up the lead and securing it in his grip. He turned to Elizabeth and Charles and bowed. "I am terribly sorry for my beastly animal! I assure you, he is a gentle giant, not vicious in the least."

He straightened and bowed once more. "John Blandishman, at your service."

Charles returned the bow. "Charles Bingley. This is my sister, Miss Elizabeth Bennet."

"I am pleased to make your acquaintance," Mr Blandishman said. "I am sorry if Griswold frightened either of you. Might you allow me to make amends? Perhaps I could extend a dinner invitation."

"We are not socialising at the moment," Charles confessed, "but once my wife is well, we would be happy to accept."

Mr Blandishman nodded in understanding and handed Charles his card. "My direction," he said. "Send word when you are available. Now, I best get this monster home! Next time, I shall send him with the footman. Mr Bingley, Miss Bennet, I bid you good day." He bowed again, and Elizabeth noticed his gaze linger on her as she curtseyed in return.

"Well, that was a fortuitous meeting," Charles remarked, offering his arm to Elizabeth.

"How so?" she asked, taking it.

Charles grinned, mischief dancing in his eyes as he spoke. "I was just lamenting that you have had little by way of socialising. Mother Bennet's nerves will be all aflutter if she discovers we made the acquaintance of a gentleman during a walk. We shall have to accept his offer to dine as soon as we are able."

Elizabeth laughed and raised her brow at Charle's jest. "Only when Jane is well," she insisted. Charles nodded, still smiling, and they walked on.

She mused over the man they had just met—Mr John Blandishman. The name seemed to suit him, as his appearance lacked vibrancy. Clad mostly in monochromatic attire, with ordinary features, he was far from striking. Sandy brown hair and mud-coloured eyes did nothing to lend him distinction. She could only hope his personality would prove more engaging than his outward appearance suggested.

She scolded herself lightly, acknowledging that her thoughts of Mr Darcy were affecting her opinion of this new acquaintance. It was rather foolish, really—the master of the Lake House could look as toadish as her cousin Collins!

Later that evening, Elizabeth finally sat to pen her reply to Mr Darcy. Exhaustion loosened her tongue—or rather, her pen—and she wrote more candidly than she typically would and poured her heart out to the gentleman from the past. It was well into the early hours when she sealed the letter. She resolved to place it on the salver in the morning, then went to her bed and fell into a deep sleep.

Chapter Seven

July 25, 1810
The Lake House
Ramsgate
Darcy

Darcy held Miss Bennet's letter in hand, feeling both relief and irritation at the delay. As he broke the seal, he noticed discolouration along the edges—a sign that someone had opened and resealed it. He broke the seal, unfolded the paper, and a scrap fell to the floor. Leaning down, he picked it up and began to read.

July 24, 1812

Dear Sir,
I must apologise for the delay. Several nights ago, I penned a reply to your letter, intending to place it on the salver with the outgoing post the next morning. In my haste to attend my sister, the letter fell behind the table. By the time I found it, the salver was already overflowing, so I set it aside, only to discover the servants had left it untouched. I write this

brief note by way of explanation and enclose it with my original missive. Pray, sir, forgive the delay.

E. Bennet

Darcy set aside the note and opened Miss Bennet's latest letter, eager to read what she had to say.

July 20, 1812

Dear Mr Darcy,

It pleases me to report that the coin you secreted under the seal remained intact when I opened your letter. Your playful nature is surely not something you reveal to just anyone, and I am flattered that you have shared this side of yourself with me. Following your example, I have likewise secured a coin under the seal; note the date and marvel at the remarkable situation in which we find ourselves entangled.

As for the snuffbox hidden in the hollow tree, it has remained undetected this long and I am confident that it will continue to do so until your sister retrieves it.

My practise at your sister's music continues apace. I grow better with each playing. Soon, my brother will cease to cover his ears at my poor attempts, and I shall be able to delight the room with my efforts without giving my relations cause to blush.

Your sister sounds like a veritable paragon! How much she must be required to learn as a young lady of the first circles! I am grateful to my father for always providing his daughters with any masters they requested, as well as books and education whenever we pursued knowledge. Yet I have never received the instruction your sister likely has. There were no ladies' seminaries for me and mine. Jane and I never felt the lack, nor, I suppose, did Mary, who is by far the most dedicated to her studies amongst the Bennet sisters. Kitty and Lydia, however, have not applied themselves, and with my mother's approval, they spend much of their time in idleness. Lydia can decorate a bonnet, and Kitty can draw passably, but I do believe neither is prepared to manage a household of her own.

Here I am rambling on about my family's foibles, despite having assured you I would not bore you with such details! No matter. It is too late now to begin this missive anew. I can only hope that you laugh upon reading my descriptions, rather than furrow your brow in utter disdain.

Your gentlemanlike reply to my self-deprecating remarks is most impressive. I find it difficult to argue with such sensible words. It pleases me greatly that you wish to continue exchanging letters with this impertinent miss. I only hope you do not become weary of me!

The Lake House is indeed a lovely place. I can well imagine spending summers here, away from the heat of town. The sound of the waves would surely have lulled me to sleep whilst also tempting me to escape my nurses and run to the shore. My poor mama despaired of me, you know, for I was always returning to the house with soiled hems and mud upon my gowns. I must admit, as I have grown older, little has changed.

The garden here is nearly perfect, lacking only lavender to make it so. Upon my arrival, I admit I was sorely disappointed to find my favourite bloom absent amidst the many other beautiful blossoms. Longbourn boasts an extensive array of flora and fauna, yet the lavender field has always delighted me. As lavender serves so many uses, we keep an ample supply in the stillroom, and the estate provides the local apothecary and villagers with whatever they require.

What must you have been like as a little boy? You have yet to describe yourself, so I must conjure an image. Surely, you were tall, with knobby knees and gangly limbs. I cannot imagine your nurse allowing you to be anything less than impeccably attired, so you were likely a miniature gentleman. I dare not speculate further upon your features, lest I unintentionally offend you.

Life in Hertfordshire gives me no reason to repine. Our small community granted me greater freedom than one might enjoy living in London. My papa endures the six females in his household much as you imagined your own father would have—hiding in his study, joining us only for meals and occasionally socialising. His genuine passion lies with his books, and he surrounds himself with the written word whenever possible.

Though I love him dearly, I cannot overlook his lack of engagement with his children. Papa is, at best, disinterested and, at worst, neglectful, though he has always ensured that we are well provided for with the necessities of life. We have food on the table and clothing to wear, yet, as I have mentioned, my younger sisters are verging on wild, for he refuses to take the trouble of checking their behaviour. I love my sisters dearly, but they can indeed be a sore trial.

I now take considerable pleasure in informing you that we share yet another connexion. You revealed it in your last letter, and I wish I could witness your expression upon reading my next words.

Let me begin by answering one of your questions. There is an entail on my father's estate, and a distant cousin is the heir. His name is William Collins, and I have never met a more nonsensical man! Last year, he took orders, and almost immediately had the remarkable honour of securing a valuable family living. His patroness is none other than Lady Catherine de Bourgh of Rosings Park, Kent. Are you not diverted?

You know your aunt well enough to accurately predict my cousin's disposition. He is a sycophant, combining an odd mixture of pomposity, condescension, and false humility. The man appeared on Longbourn's doorstep last autumn, determined to make a match with one of his 'fair cousins.' Imagine his dismay when he discovered that the eldest and most *beautiful was already well on her way to forming an attachment with the new occupant of Netherfield Park.*

At my mother's urging, he turned his attentions to me, and after less than a se'ennight in his company, he declared himself to me. Since you address me as Miss Bennet and not Mrs Collins, you can easily surmise my reply. I remain eternally grateful to my dear father for not forcing me to accept him.

In the end, he married my particular friend, Miss Charlotte Lucas. After visiting them this past Easter, I observed that she seems content with her new role as mistress of her own household. Charlotte was nearly on the shelf, you see, and I believe she viewed this as an opportunity to secure her independence from her family.

I had the dubious honour of dining 'nine' times at Rosings Park whilst in Kent. Mrs Collins's sister meticulously kept count of our invitations, and she wasted no time informing all of Meryton upon our return.

As I imagine you may be eager to know my opinion of your esteemed aunt, I shall not hesitate to oblige. Lady Catherine is as subtle as a stampeding horse. She interrogated me with all manner of intrusive questions, and I daresay I vexed her greatly with my replies; I was not particularly forthcoming.

Your cousin Anne scarcely spoke, thus offering me little to remark upon. Lady Catherine, however, bemoaned her daughter's unmarried state, repeating a particular refrain at least four times: 'Anne's fate is sealed. If not for... well, it does not bear speaking of. But now she will never marry.' This remark intrigues me anew, especially in light of current circumstances. Perhaps by 1812, you have disabused her of the notion that you will ever marry her daughter.

There is yet another connexion I must disclose. You mention your estate lies near the village of Lambton. Coincidentally, my Aunt Gardiner spent much of her youth there. I intend to write to her directly to learn of more details. It is within the realm of possibility that you and she may have crossed paths in the past.

Your description of Pemberley was much appreciated. I can almost envision it. My Aunt Gardiner has often expressed a desire to revisit the village of her youth, and perhaps I may convince her to take me along. Should that occur, I might be so bold as to request a tour of your estate from your housekeeper, especially now that you have revealed the grandeur of your library. I confess, I am exceedingly fond of reading and always reserve a portion of my trunk for my favourite volumes. However, I am pleased with what the Lake House offers, and my own books lie forgotten in the depths of my luggage as I peruse the shelves here.

I ought to scold you for your continued insistence that this strange distortion of time has not occurred on your behalf, for who better to receive such an extraordinary experience than the scion of an earl? My family is far below yours in status; though you are a gentleman, and I am gentleman's daughter, my mother's roots are far humbler, a fact that would likely make your relations gasp in horror. Your cousin the colonel sounds like a lovely person, however. Would I find in him a kindred spirit, do you think?

My exhausted ramblings have filled two pages! How fortunate we are not bound by the cost of postage. Though my bed calls to me, I must answer your questions before I retire. I already addressed the entailment, so I can move to the next concern.

Jane is not well at all. She remains dreadfully ill and can barely keep more than a little broth down before casting up her accounts. My dear brother frets endlessly for her, and I must conceal my own anxiety to avoid exacerbating his. I have assured him countless times that Jane will recover, though I wonder if I am seeking to convince him or myself.

Jane believes she is near to feeling the quickening, and my aunt assures me that much of the sickness should ease thereafter. I pray it will, for my poor sister is much too thin.

As for my favourite pastimes, I am fond of reading, and I also enjoy a healthy walk. I have thoroughly explored Longbourn's lands and its surrounding environs. Whilst here in Ramsgate, my brother insists that I always take a footman with me. He is correct in his caution, but I find the lack of solitude irksome.

I am not terribly fond of riding. I can manage well enough, but I am far more at ease on my own two feet than in a saddle. As for hunting and fishing, I do not partake in either, finding them less appealing than other pursuits.

My mother despairs of me, for I do not favour the more ladylike pursuits she holds in high regard. I play the pianoforte passably well, as I have mentioned, but my embroidery is less than refined, and I do not draw or paint tables. Netting purses holds no interest, nor do I take pleasure in arranging flowers or redecorating bonnets. I prefer to be active and useful, and thus, I spend my time in the still room or visiting tenants.

It is nearing midnight now, and I must close. Please forgive the excessive length of this letter.

Sincerely,

E. Bennet

Darcy folded the letter carefully, removing the coin from beneath the wax as he did so. He ran his thumb over its surface, noting the year 1812 stamped upon it. After finishing the fold, he held the missive in his hand, his eyes tracing the feminine script on the front. It was indeed a rather long letter, but he was glad for it. Each word revealed more about Miss Elizabeth Bennet, offering him further insight into her character. Like her, he began to conjure images of the lady in his mind. Was her hair brown or blond? Perhaps it was red or black. Were her eyes bright blue, dark grey, or hazel?

Darcy shook his head, realising that imagining Miss Bennet's features would do him no good. Instead, he chuckled at the strange coincidence that her cousin was his aunt's rector. As he glanced at the letter in his hand, another idea sprouted in his mind. Rising from his chair, he rang for the footman to relay his instructions. Once that task was complete, he went in search of Georgiana. He discovered her in her sitting room, bent over a history book, her tongue poking out slightly as she concentrated.

"Hello, dearest," he greeted, startling her.

"Brother!" Her face lit up, and she straightened, closing the book. "What brings you here?"

"I wondered if you might like to practise your drawing today," he said carefully. "What say you to attempting my portrait?"

She grinned widely. "Yes, I would! The drawing master at my seminary was quite skilled. I believe you will not be disappointed if you sit for me."

"Then let us go to it!" Darcy grinned back, gesturing for her to accompany him. "The light will be better in the parlour." Georgiana eagerly followed him, and Darcy, feeling rather pleased with himself, thought that Miss Bennet would receive not one, but two surprises in his next letter.

Chapter Eight

July 30, 1812
The Lake House
Ramsgate
Elizabeth

Elizabeth closed the door to Jane's bedchamber softly, careful not to disturb her sleeping sister. Over the past five days, Jane's condition had seen a dramatic improvement, and earlier that day she had even managed to stomach a bit of toast without feeling ill. The hopeful expression on Charles's face remained imprinted in Elizabeth's mind, his pure love and adoration for her sister displayed for all to see.

Jane's strength had not returned, although she was now awake for longer periods than she had been the previous weeks. Charles remained by his wife's side, and when he could not, Elizabeth would take his place in the chair next to Jane's bed, reading or embroidering half-heartedly as her sister slept. She even added some lace to the fine baby gown Jane had completed before the sickness had fully taken hold.

Eager to be out of doors and disinclined to the company of a footman, Elizabeth made her way to the garden at the rear of the house.

Large enough for a solitary walk, it would provide the quiet she craved. Donning her bonnet and half-boots, she slipped through the door and into the midst of the summer blooms.

The garden paths were familiar now, and Elizabeth soon reached her favourite spot—the stone bench beneath the tree that concealed the snuffbox. As she rounded the bend, she froze, her mouth falling open in shock.

Lining the wall on either side of the tree were rows of lavender! A quick count revealed ten plants, each in full bloom. Her heart warmed at the sight, and she approached cautiously, almost fearful that if she blinked, the plants might vanish.

Drawing nearer, she bent to tenderly brush the purple blooms with her fingers. Their fragrance rose on the breeze, and she breathed deeply, savouring the heady aroma. Carefully, she picked a bundle of the herbaceous flowers to take with her into the house.

With the gathered lavender in her hand, Elizabeth hesitated before returning to the house and sank onto the bench, her gaze wandering around the garden as her thoughts drifted to Mr Darcy. What sort of man would add a stranger's favourite bloom to his garden simply on a whim? Surely, he had done so after receiving her last letter, for the lavender had not been present when she had last sought sanctuary in the garden.

Elizabeth enjoyed sketching characters and Mr Darcy had become a fascinating study—a puzzle she could only piece together through his letters. After his first, she had labelled him haughty, egotistical, and arrogant, but she had long since amended her opinion of him. Mr Darcy was kind, intelligent, and possessed a bit of humour and whimsy. He seemed to be a dedicated brother and master, too.

Elizabeth started, realising that she ought to guard her heart, for what she knew of Mr Darcy spelled danger. It would take but little effort to fall completely and irrevocably in love with him. What folly it would be to lose her heart to a man in the past! Such heavy thoughts required more reflection, and the confines of the back garden offered little relief. Rising from the bench, she felt an overwhelming restlessness. Her steps carried her swiftly through the shrubs and blooms back to the house, where she rang for a footman to accompany her to the park. Elizabeth handed the lavender to a maid and requested she put it in water and place it in her chamber.

James and John stood waiting by the door as Elizabeth tied her bonnet. John stepped forward to open the door, following her out into the warm summer air. She set a brisk pace, and John, keeping a respectful distance, allowed the illusion of being alone.

Her thoughts were in turmoil as she neared the park. Was she mad to be corresponding with a man so wholly unconnected to her? If someone ever discovered their letters, it would utterly ruin her reputation, whilst Mr Darcy, safe in the past, would remain beyond the reach of her father.

And what of the thoughts that had come to her in the garden? If she were to lose her heart to Mr Darcy of Pemberley, how could they ever meet? Would he appear suddenly in her life, at some inauspicious moment—perhaps when she had entered a courtship with another? Where was Mr Darcy in her time? Could he already be married? Why else would he lease the Lake House, when he claimed he had never done so before?

Her feet carried her to the far end of the park, where another gate led to a different street. As she approached it, a familiar figure came through. Mr Blandishman called out to her cheerfully.

"Miss Bennet! I have walked the park daily hoping to encounter you." He stepped forward and bowed, grinning broadly as he straightened. "You need not fear for your safety today, as I left Griswold behind."

Elizabeth smiled and returned his greeting. "How do you do, Mr Blandishman?"

"I am very well, thank you. Might I have the pleasure of joining you on your stroll?"

He looked so eager that Elizabeth could not bring herself to deny him. "I would be pleased to walk with you, sir. John, my footman, will accompany us." She glanced at the burly servant, whose face bore a slight scowl. After a moment, John nodded.

Mr Blandishman tugged at his cravat. "Very good," he said, offering his arm. Elizabeth took it, mindful to keep a proper distance between them.

"I had nearly given up hope I would see you again. That is, I know your brother was to send his card, but I had hoped that we might meet before then..." he trailed off into silence.

Elizabeth smiled to herself at the man's awkwardness. "My sister improves with each passing day," she replied. "She is able to eat more now, and I believe within a few weeks she will be well enough to venture out."

"And is the entire household eschewing guests whilst the mistress convalesces?" Mr Blandishman shuffled his feet as they walked, causing Elizabeth to narrow her eyes slightly at his question. Why was he so interested in social calls?

"I only mean to say that I would like the opportunity to come to know you better," he added hastily. "And your brother, of course—but mostly you. I confess I do not wish to wait several weeks to become better acquainted."

Ah, so that was the rub. He wished to call upon *her*. Elizabeth felt an inexplicable distaste for the idea, her thoughts drifting towards Mr

Darcy and their continued correspondence. Mr Darcy was far more engaging than Mr Blandishman.

Immediately, she chastised herself. It was unfair to judge Mr Blandishman so early in their acquaintance. Had she not done the same with Mr Darcy after his first letters? In truth, she knew little of Mr Blandishman.

Besides, Mr Darcy was not here—Mr Blandishman was. For all Elizabeth knew, whatever strange occurrences had allowed her to correspond with Mr Darcy across time might not last. She was beneath him in station; was it so unlikely that by 1812, he might have a titled, well-dowered wife, and possibly a child?

"I believe my brother will not object to receiving callers," she said carefully. "Mr Bingley is an amiable man and fond of company. He is often at home."

Mr Blandishman favoured her with a wide smile, and once more, Elizabeth noticed just how ordinary his appearance was. He was not so poorly favoured as Mr Collins, but she imagined there would be a greater resemblance if Mr Blandishman sported the same sycophantic smile her cousin often wore. Could Mr Darcy be equally plain?

They walked on, with Mr Blandishman bearing the bulk of the conversation. Elizabeth attempted to focus, but the gentleman was, simply put, dull. He spoke at length of his house in Ramsgate and the improvements he was making. She might have shown some interest had he not delved into such excruciating detail. His conversation was too reminiscent of Mr Collins, further deepening her aversion towards the gentleman. He also spoke of his dog, Griswold. Elizabeth was not fond of dogs and felt horrified to learn that Mr Blandishman owned *three* of the enormous creatures—and that they roamed freely about his house.

After some time, she said, "I must turn back now, sir. My brother will expect me for tea."

"Of course," Mr Blandishman replied, bowing as he released her arm. "Might I ask when you plan to walk again? I would be happy to accompany you."

"I have no notion of when I might next venture out," she answered firmly. "Today was a spur-of-the-moment decision. Until Jane is well, my walks will be scarce, I fear."

"Then I shall come to the park every day, hoping to meet you," he said, his words striking Elizabeth as an awkward attempt at romance. Instead, Mr Blandishman's words rendered him somewhat... Was there even a word for it? *Off-putting*?

"Your time is yours to spend as you will." Her voice remained even, giving him no encouragement. It seemed he was already thinking of an attachment after only two meetings. Once more, Elizabeth felt the situation was far too reminiscent of Mr Collins for her liking, and she resolved she must know him much better before even considering the idea of courtship.

"I am sure my brother will send his card should there be a day he is available to receive company," she said, dipping a curtsey before turning away. John fell into step behind her, and once they had covered a distance, she sighed loudly.

"If you do not care for his company, simply say so, Miss Bennet," John said in a muted but firm tone. "I will not tolerate a gent poking his nose where 'tis not wanted. Too many are hurt when that happens."

"Thank you, John," Elizabeth replied sincerely. "I am still forming my opinion of him, though he seems quite certain I am worth pursuing. I will inform you if I no longer wish for his company."

"Very good, madam." John fell silent but stayed close as they returned to the Lake House. Elizabeth wondered at his protective nature and what had spurred it.

Charles dined with Jane late that evening, and though he invited Elizabeth to join them, she declined, feeling unequal to the company after the disruption of her peaceful walk. Instead, she ordered a tray sent up to her chamber and thrilled at the discovery of another letter from Mr Darcy in the day's post. She eagerly broke the seal, her heart lifting as she saw the letter was just as long as the one she had written. After casting a glance at the lavender in the vase on her dressing table, she settled into her chair to devour the latest words from the past.

July 24, 1810

Dear Miss Bennet,
Pray forgive the delay in my reply. I wished to complete two tasks before writing to you. The first you may already have discovered in the garden. Tell me, is there now lavender lining the wall where the stone bench stands? I know little of the plant, nor how swiftly it grows, but I trust that in two years it has blossomed from the small starts I procured into handsome plants. My servants were somewhat puzzled by my request but carried out their duties admirably. Pray, inform me if the plants have survived in your next letter.

The other matter you will learn of later. I bid you to be patient, for I will reveal all before I close this missive. So, I pen most of it now in the hope that by day's end, I shall be ready to sand and seal it with the enclosed item.

I am pleased that my coin travelled with the letter. I wonder what else we might send to each other. Could we perhaps send books or other items? Is there a limit to the size and scope of what can pass through these unexplained currents of time? I know not, and so for now, I shall content myself with small tributes.

I, too, wonder why Georgiana has not retrieved the snuffbox from its hiding place. My father has been gone these three years already; I would have thought she would have collected the memento by now. She knows I abhor snuff, so there would be no cause for me to take it.

Does your playing really cause listeners distress? I must admit, I find it difficult to determine whether you are teasing me or entirely sincere in your self-deprecating remarks. Be that as it may, I hope you master the Mozart piece, and that it brings you as much comfort as it once brought my dear sister.

Georgiana... Allow me to tell you more of her. She may not be a paragon, but I am certain that when she comes out in a few years, she will captivate the ton. *With impeccable lineage, a considerable dowry, and excellent connexions, I expect I shall be fending off suitors with a stick when the time comes. Yet, all that pales in comparison to her innate goodness, her sweetness of temper, and her kind heart.*

At fifteen, she is still just a girl, though already tall for her age. With fair hair and blue eyes, I believe she will resemble our mother even more in the years to come. She is quiet and shy, much like her elder brother. Before you laugh at my use of 'shy' for myself, let me assure you that, as a boy of fifteen, it suited me well. I was tall and awkward, my voice prone to cracking, and I often held my silence, particularly in the company of my peers. Now, I would say I am merely reserved. I do hope, for your sake as well as theirs, that your sisters experience a similar transformation in the coming years. Is Jane your only sister who is wed?

Pray, do not allow me to suspend any pleasure of yours should you wish to continue to do so. I could prattle on about the foibles and faults of my family as much as you do yours. As proof, I shall regale you with more tales of my cousin, Richard. Yes, I believe you would find in him a kindred spirit, and I eagerly await your own judgement on the matter.

Colonel Richard Fitzwilliam is as fine a man as any I know. He is honest to a fault, courageous, loyal, kind, and intelligent. He is loquacious where I am quiet, and I often find company easier to bear when he is present. As a younger son, he must make his own way in the world. His brother, the heir, is competent yet unmarried. My aunt and uncle adore Richard, and I know it troubles them he is often in harm's way. Make no mistake: they love him as more than just the 'spare,' but the responsibility of continuing the family line is ever-present, since their eldest has no son of his own at this time.

Richard has always been a stalwart companion, from our youth through Eton and university. He defended me when the sons of peers attempted to disparage me, and our bond has remained steadfast. He also stood by me when a childhood friend tried to tarnish my reputation and have me sent down from school. If it were not for Richard's timely presentation of evidence corroborating my story, that former friend might have succeeded.

Ah, I have become maudlin. It pains me to recall that particular individual. He was the son of my father's steward and my father's godson, and thus, we spent much of our youth together, even attending school side by side. As we grew older, however, he began to resent my position as heir. I believe he wished to supplant me in my father's affections, hoping to benefit from his godfather's generosity as much as possible. In the end, my father bequeathed him one thousand pounds, along with the offer of a valuable family living, should he choose to take orders. He accepted the money, but the living is yet to fall vacant. Impatient, he declared his disinterest in taking orders and expressed a desire to study the law instead. We eventually agreed on a sum of three thousand pounds for the living. It was a fortunate decision—his conduct at university was not befitting a clergyman. I do not know what he has been doing these three years past.

Richard is best suited to tell you what I was like as a boy. He would likely claim that I was always well-behaved and never gave my parents cause for displeasure. He would be mistaken, of course. I have already acquainted you with one of my youthful escapades, but I assure you, there were many more. Your imaginings are close to the truth—I did indeed have knobby knees and gangly limbs until I reached my full height. I stand at six feet two inches. Though I now wear my cravat and coat as expected of a gentleman, I did not always dress impeccably, and even at sixteen, I often discarded them. My tolerance for such garments has not improved with age.

I cannot fathom having the liberty to wander freely as you did. Even as a young man, my father insisted a footman or groom accompany me whenever I ventured out. How different it must have been for you, a young lady, to enjoy such independence. A part of me is inclined to criticise your father for his laxity in your care, but you strike me as a woman who knows her own mind and does not easily bend to the will of others. Had your father attempted to rein you in, would you have obeyed?

Now, I wish to address both 'connexions' you have listed. You cannot imagine my astonishment upon reading that my aunt, in your time, appointed your cousin as rector for the Hunsford parish! No doubt I shall meet him at some point during one of my visits to Rosings Park. It perplexes me we did not cross paths at Easter in 1812, as I traditionally visit at that time to inspect my aunt's estate. What kept me away remains a mystery. Perhaps your supposition is correct, and I have somehow earned my aunt's displeasure. I can almost hear her saying, with her usual imperious air, "I am most seriously displeased."

I can well envision Mr Collins and his character. My aunt surrounds herself with those who flatter her and indulge her with excessive compliments. *The false humility, pomposity, and condescension you describe suggests that your cousin fits this mould perfectly. My aunt is surely pleased with her new toadeater.*

Is it poor form for me to rejoice in Mr Collins's failure to secure you for a bride? You seem far too lively a lady to be under my aunt's influence. As I am sure you noted during your visit to your friend, Aunt Catherine is excessively attentive to all within her sphere and never hesitates to direct or command as she pleases. I hope Mrs Collins possesses a stalwart disposition, for anything less than a will of iron will surely melt beneath Lady Catherine's scorching gaze.

The connexion between your aunt and the village of Lambton is astonishing. What a coincidence! Fate must indeed have a sense of humour, to entwine us so closely despite never having met. I hope to meet your aunt someday—or become reacquainted with her—should we have met before. Perhaps it will be when you accompany your relations on a tour of Pemberley.

Now comes the bit of your letter I ought to have addressed at the beginning. Please forgive me for being so remiss. How fares your sister's health? Has she improved? Your concern for her well-being is clear, and I sincerely hope, for your sake and for her husband's, that her strength returns with each passing day. Pray inform me of her condition when next you write.

Tell me more of your elder sister. Is she like you? If so, her husband must count himself fortunate indeed to have won such a wife.

I am pleased to learn that you delight in reading as much as I had supposed. Walking is another admirable pastime, and I hope you have been able to enjoy that whilst in Ramsgate. The town offers many fine prospects, and I would hate for you to miss them because of your prolonged confinement to the house.

It is late, and I must close, but before I do, I convinced my sister to sketch my likeness for you. It is a simple pencil drawing, but an accurate rendering. My hair is a dark brown, almost black, and my eyes are blue. Your imagination should now be satisfied.

I will await your next letter with anticipation.

Sincerely yours,

Fitzwilliam Darcy.

Elizabeth gazed at the sketch carefully positioned between the pages of the letter. It was wonderfully executed, capturing the striking image of a handsome man of some six-and-twenty years. His hair was slightly curled, and a soft smile graced his lips. His eyes seemed to twinkle with a hint of amusement. Miss Darcy had indeed proven herself talented in capturing such a likeness.

Elizabeth studied his handsome countenance, something about him striking her as vaguely familiar. However, she could not place where she might have encountered the gentleman before. "So, this is Mr Fitzwilliam Darcy of Pemberley. He is far from the ogre I imagined, and his appearance is much preferable to that of Mr Collins!" She sighed as her heart gave a small flutter. "Yes, Lizzy," she muttered to herself, "you are in real danger of losing your heart."

Ignoring her dinner tray, Elizabeth retrieved a fresh sheet of paper and began to write a reply. Once finished, she plucked a sprig of lavender from the vase on her dressing table and tucked it between the folds of her letter before sealing it.

I shall ask Jane tomorrow if she is well enough to sketch my likeness. It will be nothing to compare to Miss Darcy's work, but my sister's talent is respectable. It would not do to let Mr Darcy imagine the worst about me! Smiling happily, she finally turned to her now cold dinner, eating what she could. A while later, Elizabeth slipped the letter into her writing case and climbed into bed before snuffing out her candle. That night, her dreams were filled with the face she now knew belonged to the very handsome Fitzwilliam Darcy.

Chapter Nine

August 3, 1810
The Lake House
Ramsgate
Darcy

The afternoon sun shone through the study window, raising the temperature in the room beyond Darcy's comfort. He rose from his desk and crossed the room, unlatched the window, and pushed it open. A welcome breeze offered relief, carrying with it the salty scent of the sea. The soothing rhythm of the waves crashing against the shore, mixed with the occasional cry of seabirds overhead, filled the air with a sense of tranquillity. Darcy breathed deeply, taking in the calming sounds and scents of the ocean.

The door opened behind him, and Smythe announced, "George Wickham to see you, sir."

Darcy stiffened, and fixing his expression into an impassive mask, he turned to confront his visitor.

"Wickham," he said tersely. "What an unexpected... surprise."

His childhood companion flashed that familiar, cheeky grin—the same smile that had charmed ladies and deceived gentlemen alike over the years. Darcy felt the urge to erase it from his face. "Come now, Darcy," Wickham said with an exaggerated air. "Is that how you greet your oldest friend?"

"Our business concluded three years ago. Why are you here?"

Wickham hesitated a bit before he drew closer to the desk. "Might I sit?" he asked, his tone dripping with false humility.

"If you must." Darcy moved to his own chair, sitting with his back rigid, a faint frown tugging at his lips. "What brings you to Ramsgate?"

The chair creaked as Wickham shifted in his seat. His expression turned contrite, his gaze dropping to his shoes. After clearing his throat, he spoke. "I have heard rumours that the incumbent of the Kympton living means to retire by the end of the year."

How had Wickham heard that? Darcy wondered briefly. *He must still have friends in Lambton.* "And what of it?" he said aloud.

"I wish to be granted the living." Wickham's gaze rose to meet his, determination etched in his expression. "My situation is dire, and I believe that I am suited to the church, after all."

"No."

Wickham's shock was palpable. Had he truly expected Darcy to respond differently?

"Is this all the reply I am to receive?" His tone carried incredulity, and Darcy nearly laughed at the absurdity of the situation.

"What more needs saying? I have it in writing that you relinquished all claims to the living in exchange for three thousand pounds. That, combined with your inheritance from my father, ought to have secured your future—had you invested wisely and lived within your means. Your behaviour gives me no reason to grant you the position of spiritual advisor for the parish of Kympton."

Wickham scowled. "Your father would be ashamed of you," he spat, his voice filled with venom. "I was like a son to him. How can you cast me aside so easily?"

Darcy rose from his chair, towering over his former friend. The barb about his father stung, but he had long made peace with George Darcy's blindness when it came to his godson. "My father would be ashamed of *you*," he countered firmly. "You abandoned every principle he instilled in us and squandered every privilege he bestowed. You received a gentleman's education, yet you have wasted it! No, Wickham, your misfortunes are entirely of your making, and you will not bully me into offering you the living out of some misguided loyalty to my father. Tell me, what became of your study of the law?"

Wickham's frown deepened, and he looked away. "It did not suit," he muttered.

"Why does that not surprise me?" Darcy's sarcasm earned him a venomous glare, but he ignored it. "I will offer you one last opportunity," he continued, moving deliberately around the desk. "I will help you secure honest employment at a reputable firm or warehouse. If, after three years, you have proven your constancy and dedication, I will consider aiding you further. If you refuse, then our dealings are at an end, and I shall have nothing more to do with you."

Wickham shot to his feet, his fists clenched at his sides. "This is not over, Darcy," he hissed. "You will regret this slight. I will have my revenge on you and your family for this lack of consideration."

Darcy walked to the bellpull and summoned Smythe. "Good day, Wickham. I wish you success in your future endeavours." The butler opened the door and turned to his master for directions. "Mr Wickham is leaving," he informed the servant. The butler stepped forward to escort him out, only for Wickham to jerk his arm away forcefully.

"I have warned you, Darcy," he growled as he strode towards the door, Smythe following closely behind.

Darcy held his breath until he heard the front door close, and the lock click into place. "Thank heaven he is gone," he muttered, sinking into his chair with a weary sigh. He ran a hand over his face, the tension finally lessening.

"The post, sir," Smythe announced as he re-entered the room, extending a stack of letters. Darcy accepted them absently, barely registering when his butler left, closing the door softly behind him.

He sorted through the pile, setting aside invitations and bills, before his attention settled on *two* letters from Elizabeth—he shook his head. *No, not Elizabeth. Miss Bennet.* He ought not to think of her so familiarly. He opened the thicker letter first, startled as a 'fresh' sprig of lavender slipped from between the pages and landed on his desk. He picked it up, inhaling the soothing fragrance before setting it aside and turning his focus eagerly to her words.

July 31, 1812

Dear Mr Darcy,

Imagine my overwhelming astonishment, sir, as I strolled in your lovely garden earlier today only to view flowers that were not there the day before. I could scarcely believe my eyes, yet there they were—ten lavender plants, fully in bloom. A vase full of the blossoms is now set beside me as I write. Thank you. Your kindness humbles me—no one has ever done something so thoughtful for me. Do tell, was the sprig I enclosed still fresh, or did it wither as it crossed the barrier of time and space?

Added to that surprise, was the pleasant appearance of your likeness enclosed with your letter. I must say, there is much to admire, and you look nothing like the ogre I had imagined. From your first letter, I pictured a figure with long fangs and a dreadful scowl, but the reality is definitely an improvement over my fanciful imaginings. I shall endeavour not to inflate your pride, but I must say, I have never seen a more well-favoured gentleman in my life.

As for Jane, she is feeling much better, and we believe the worst is behind her. She is awake more often now and is taking more nourishment each day. We hope that within a week or so, she will leave her chamber entirely.

You asked me to tell you more about my sister, and I am most happy to oblige. Jane is an angel, sent to Earth to show us mere mortals the true meaning of goodness. In nearly all cases, she sees only the good in people and desires that those around her exhibit the same kindness and compassion she so naturally possesses. Her ladylike conduct has been an example to all her sisters, and it is only through her gentle guidance—and that of our dear Aunt Gardiner that I did not grow into a complete hoyden. If there ever was an impoverished gentleman's daughter who deserved to marry well, it is Jane. Fortunately, she is completely smitten with her husband, and he with her.

Jane's improvement allows me the freedom to venture out more often. Twice now, I have encountered a gentleman during my walks. The first meeting was memorable, for he had a large black dog with him that was very interested in me and my brother-in-law. On the second occasion, Mr Blandishman was alone. I am not fond of dogs, so I was relieved he left the creature at home.

My brother will send his card around to the gentleman when Jane is well enough to entertain. Mr Blandishman has invited us to dine but has kindly agreed to wait upon my sister's recovery. In the meantime, he has expressed a desire to visit me at the Lake House. His interest is unmistakable, and I am endeavouring not to dismiss him without a reason. It is only that he is so very... well, he is nothing like you or my brother.

Shall I describe him to you? Pray, be so good as to inform me if you wish for a description.

I have had a letter from my father. You would not know this, but it is a rare occurrence. Papa is not a faithful correspondent, and upon opening it, I presumed he was writing to beg me to come home. I was not entirely wrong; he lamented my absence, complained about my mother and sisters, and declared that with both me and Jane gone, Longbourn has been devoid of rational discourse for weeks.

He also tells me that Lydia has gone off to Brighton with her 'particular friend,' Mrs Forster, the young wife of the colonel of the regiment recently stationed in Meryton. The presence of the officers provided a boon to the local merchants and a 'delightful' diversion for the young ladies of the area. Do you detect my sarcasm? For months, my two youngest sisters had nothing to speak of but officers, and it grew rather tedious to remain in the same room as Kitty and Lydia.

How long do you stay in Ramsgate during the summers? I imagine that, as a landowner, it is necessary for you to attend to your estate during the harvest and spring planting. From your words, I gather you are a diligent master and oversee matters at Pemberley yourself, rather than relying entirely on a steward. Will you be journeying north to Derbyshire soon?

Your sentiments about my cousin Collins's failure to secure my hand echo my own, I assure you. Mama was furious at my refusal; by me marrying the heir to my father's estate, her future would have been secure. She does not understand when I explain that I desire more than mere security in life. I have witnessed my father's unfeeling treatment of his wife, and though my mother is not clever enough to fully grasp his barbs, she knows he mocks her. I have seen the hurt in her eyes, and I have *no wish to enter into such an unequal union. I shall marry for love, and nothing less, just as Jane has done. Her husband is everything he ought to be—handsome, amiable, kind... that he is also rich had no bearing on her decision, I promise.*

Would it not be interesting if you knew my dear aunt when she lived in Lambton? Her maiden name was Partridge; does that aid you as you search your memories? I will have to tell you of the Gardiners when I next write, but I am tired, and my candle is burning low. My dinner sits cold on a tray beside me, forgotten in my haste to read your missive. I have fallen into a dreadful habit of writing letters into the wee hours of the morning, and I shall suffer a megrim if I do not make my way to bed soon.

Will you tell me more of your family? You said little of your parents, other than that they are no longer living.

I do hope your day is a pleasant one.

Sincerely,

E. Bennet

Darcy sighed. If only his day had been pleasant. He set the letter aside and picked up the other, much lighter missive. He broke the seal and read the brief note at the top of the page.

August 2, 1812

Dear Sir,

It is only fair that I grant you the same courtesy that you have bestowed upon me. Behold, a passable likeness of one Miss Elizabeth Bennet, rendered by my dear sister Jane as she lay abed. Jane is not as gifted artistically as Miss Darcy, but the likeness is accurate enough to give you some idea of my appearance. My hair is a riotous mess of dark brown curls, touched with hints of red that grow more noticeable in the summer. My eyes are dark, too, brown with a hint of green. Of my stature, I will tell you I am the shortest of the Bennet ladies.

I bid you farewell for now, sir, for I am to attend my brother as he goes to the shops.

E. Bennet

Darcy hungrily absorbed Miss Bennet's likeness, his eyes tracing every line. Her sister had done fine work, though the sketch was not as detailed as Georgiana's. Miss Bennet's eyes sparkled on the page; she seemed to be looking right at him, and he could not tear his gaze away. She was not a conventional beauty, but there was a distinct loveliness about her that made his heart stutter.

I am falling in love with her, he realised with a start. When the expected abhorrence of the idea did not immediately follow his epiphany, he paused to consider. Could he love Miss Bennet, a penniless country girl from Hertfordshire? And if he could, would he condescend to marry her?

His heart screamed *yes* to those thoughts, and he sat back, still holding her likeness in his hand. With one finger, he traced the curve of her lips and the arch of her brow. She appeared mischievous, as though she held a secret.

Yes, he was falling in love with Miss Elizabeth Bennet of Longbourn, and he had no inkling what to do about it. The matter would be simple were it not for the fact that she dwelt two years in the future. How was he to pursue the lady when he was unsure how he could even meet her in person?

Darcy's distraction lasted through dinner. Georgiana, noticing his preoccupation, tentatively asked if something was wrong, so deep in thought was he.

"I am well, Georgie," he told her in response to her inquiry. "There is a matter of some importance that I am reflecting on; nothing more. Forgive me for woolgathering and neglecting you."

She smiled. "Of course, brother," she said, returning to her meal. "I know you have many weighty matters on your mind."

If only you knew, Darcy thought.

Georgiana retired early, citing fatigue and the onset of a megrim. Darcy bid her good night, pressing a fond kiss to her cheek as she departed the dining room. With his mind still restless later that evening, Darcy donned his hat and gloves and left the house, determined to walk until he reasoned out a solution to his conundrum. How could one possibly meet a woman from the future? She could not travel back to meet him, nor could he leap forward into her time. What if she began a courtship with this Mr Blandishman before he even had the chance to meet her? The very thought filled him with unreasonable jealousy.

But... an idea struck him, and he seized upon it, determined to examine it fully before presenting it to Miss Bennet. It was so mad, so brilliant, that it just might work.

Turning back towards the Lake House, Darcy mulled over the idea, working out the particulars and crafting the details of what he would write in his next letter to Miss Bennet. It was madness—this need to meet the lady behind the letters—yet he resolved to pursue a solution until he found one.

Taking the stairs two at a time, Darcy entered his chamber, removing his coat and boots. Yanking at his cravat, which felt as though it were strangling him, he tossed it aside and took his seat at the desk and reached for a sheet of paper. Dipping his quill into the ink, he tapped off the excess. His pen hovered over the page, his thoughts churning. But then, resolute, he began to write. He wrote until the clock chimed midnight before his cramped fingers forced him to set the quill aside and finish the letter in the morning.

 Exhausted, he prepared for bed and climbed beneath the coverlet. As he closed his eyes, visions of the lovely Elizabeth swirled through his mind, lingering as he drifted into sleep.

Chapter Ten

August 6, 1812
The Lake House
Ramsgate
Elizabeth

It was with grand celebration and abject relief that Mrs Bingley joined her husband and sister for dinner in the dining room for the first time since they had taken residence at the Lake House. Charles could not contain his happiness and grinned broadly for the servants to see. Elizabeth's heart warmed at this display of her brother-in-law's deep affection for his wife, and she readily joined him in toasting Jane's restored health.

Jane's recovery progressed rapidly after that initial venture from her chambers. Her cheeks regained their rosy hue, and her hair returned to its former lustre. A small, but unmistakable swell now showed at Jane's middle, just discernable under the folds of her gown, and Elizabeth often observed her sister gently resting her hand there, a contented smile playing on her lips.

With her sister's return to health, Charles felt compelled to pen a note to Mr Blandishman, informing him they were now free to dine on whichever evening he deemed convenient. Mr Blandishman had visited the Lake House once or twice over the past weeks, at Charles's invitation. The company of another gentleman had clearly done her brother good; though Elizabeth considered herself sociable, Charles's need for society far surpassed her own.

Elizabeth's first impression of Mr Blandishman, much to her vexation and satisfaction, proved to be accurate. She was vexed because she had hoped to be mistaken. The gentleman was perfectly acceptable but dreadfully dull. Her satisfaction stemmed from the knowledge that her powers of perception were not so deficient as she had feared, especially after her misjudgement of Mr Darcy.

Oh... Mr Darcy. Her thoughts turned to him often, and now that she could hold a rendering of his handsome face in her hands, it was no longer just his words that filled her dreams. Each time she closed her eyes, the pencil sketch came to life. She wondered at the timbre of his voice. Was it deep, like Papa's, or perhaps higher in tone, like her brother's? Or maybe it fell somewhere in between. Whatever it might be, the voice in her dreams was soothing, smooth as butter and sweet as honey. The thought of him whispering sweet nothings sent chills down her spine, setting her heart racing.

Logic warred with these fantastical imaginings, reminding her she had never met the gentleman, and that falling in love with a spectre was hardly sensible. Mr Blandishman, her mind insisted, was the safer choice. He was here, in person, and despite his dull personality, he represented a prudent match for the penniless daughter of a country gentleman. Still, she would stand by her resolution to marry for nothing less than the deepest love. If she could not find that with Mr Blandishman, then she would not accept his hand.

Through his inquiries and Mr Blandishman's own accounts, Charles had learned that he not only owned his house in Ramsgate but also a small estate in Wiltshire, called Blandings. It yielded an income of around twenty-five hundred pounds a year. With no brothers or sisters, and his parents long deceased, his estate boasted several tenant farms and supported a thriving, albeit newly established, horse breeding business.

On the surface, everything seemed ideal. Mr Blandishman made no secret of his interest in Elizabeth and requested permission to call several days a week so that they might better come to know one another. Charles made it clear to Mr Blandishman that Elizabeth would never accept a marriage proposal for anything less than love. After several weeks, the gentleman expressed his desire to pursue a formal courtship, but Elizabeth had to inform him directly that, although she valued their acquaintance, it could not lead to anything more. Disappointed though he was, Mr Blandishman had no wish to sever ties with the residents of the Lake House, and so Charles tentatively agreed to allow him to continue calling—so long as he respected Elizabeth's wishes.

The more time she spent with him, the more she found Mr Blandishman's personality eerily similar to that of Mr Collins. He expressed interest in the oddest things and frequently made comments that left her blushing. For example, during one of their walks, they encountered a lady coming from the opposite direction whose appearance was rather unfortunate. She had a hawk-like nose, a narrow face, and wore a gown of an unflattering shade of puce that made her complexion appear sallow. Her bonnet was so large it seemed to swallow her whole. Mr Blandishman, to Elizabeth's mortification, was not discreet in his observations. He loudly commented on the lady's appearance, marvelling at the unfortunate creature she seemed to be. Elizabeth had flushed in mortification and cast the lady an apologetic glance before hurrying the man away. The lady had merely shrugged, her sad eyes downcast as she shuffled off down the lane.

When Elizabeth made any attempt to correct Mr Blandishman, he merely presented her with an amused chuckle and gave her a condescending pat on the hand. "Be not dismayed, my dear Miss Bennet," he had said, sounding so much like Mr Collins that she wondered if they were related. "The lady has certainly heard such things before, poor thing. If she has not, it is high time that someone informs her of her unfortunate appearance."

"It is not our place to do so," Elizabeth responded firmly. "We do not know the lady and ought not to judge her based solely on her appearance. For all we know, she buys what she can afford or wears cast-offs from her employer or family."

"You are far too charitable for your own good," he laughed, the sound grating on Elizabeth's ears like that of a braying donkey. She gritted her teeth and requested they return to the Lake House, pleading exhaustion.

Jane teased her about the connexion later that evening, further raising Elizabeth's ire.

"Mr Blandishman seems taken with you, Lizzy," she remarked, glancing up from her embroidery with a sly look. "Tell me, should we have the banns called?"

"Your imagination is very rapid, jumping from simple interest to matrimony in the blink of an eye. Mr Blandishman is at most an acquaintance. Did Charles not tell you I have refused to enter a courtship with him?"

Jane raised her brow. "He calls often; most mamas would consider that courting," she said. "Our mother certainly would!"

"Mr Blandishman and I are *ill-suited*," Elizabeth confessed, fiddling with the fringe on a pillow before clutching it to her chest. "He reminds me too much of Mr Collins."

Jane chortled, but when Elizabeth did not join her in laughter, she regarded her sister seriously. "Is he truly as bad as that?"

Elizabeth puffed her cheeks out and exhaled before sinking back into the plush cushions of the sofa. "He lacks our cousin's sycophancy, but he speaks down to me, as if he knows better simply because he is a man."

"Mayhap you should reveal your intelligence," Jane suggested, drawing her needle smoothly through the fabric. "Many gentlemen court flibbertigibbets with nary an original thought. If he can see your worth, his attitude may change."

Elizabeth had her doubts but nodded silently. Mr Blandishman did not strike her as the type of man who would appreciate a wife more intelligent than himself. For now, he respected her boundaries regarding their acquaintance. Should that change, she would refuse to be present when he called.

The following day, she hid in the garden when he came, and when Jane questioned her after his departure, she was unrepentant. Exasperated but amused, her sister simply handed Elizabeth the post that had arrived for her and returned to her tasks.

There were three letters today. The first was from Charlotte, and Elizabeth opened it eagerly. They were last together in April when she had visited Hunsford Parsonage for several weeks. Letters had been scarce since then.

July 30, 1812

THE LAKE HOUSE AT RAMSGATE

My dear Eliza,

I have been a neglectful friend, and I beg your pardon. Parish duties keep me busy, and Mr Collins often requires my help with his sermons. Miss de Bourgh, too, claims much of my time, and I dare not refuse her requests for company lest I upset my husband and Lady Catherine. The first I could manage, were it not for the second.

With great pleasure, I write to inform you of my suspicion that I am with child. I cannot say for certain, as I have yet to feel the quickening, but the early signs are present, and I longed to confide in someone. I have not told my mother nor my husband; you have the honour of being the first to know. I imagine a few months will reveal whether I am to be so blessed.

Is Jane much improved? Your last letter worried me, and given my current suspicions, I confess I wondered if I would suffer the same fate. Alas, aside from a bit of nausea, I am well enough thus far.

You have told me much of the Lake House, as you call it. But what of Ramsgate? Have you been able to venture out more? Pray, do tell me of the sea, for I have never seen it and I must experience it vicariously through your descriptions.

Give my regards to Jane and Mr Bingley.

Yours, etc.,

Charlotte Collins

Elizabeth smiled with pleasure and set her friend's letter aside. Imagine! Charlotte, a mother! It was most exciting, especially since it was possible that her friend might give birth to the next heir to Longbourn. Mama would be furious, and Lady Lucas exultant. Elizabeth would have to pen her best wishes to Charlotte directly.

The next letter came from Mama, filled with the expected admonishments that Elizabeth should find a husband. In her mother's eyes, it was a travesty that her next unwed daughter had reached the age of one-and-twenty and yet remained unmarried. Naturally, there was no mention of Jane's almost three-and-twenty years before she had wed.

The third letter was the one she most wished to read, and she broke the seal as quickly as she could.

August 5, 1810

Dear Miss Bennet,

Thank you for your generous gift—both the sprig of lavender and the sketch. The lavender sits proudly on my desk, and once it dries, I shall preserve it in a pouch to keep forever. As for the sketch, I have it nicely tucked away amongst my private correspondence, where only I can gaze upon your beauty. Have I shocked you, Miss Bennet, with my forward speech? Your sister Jane possesses considerable talent, and though you claim the likeness to be simple, your loveliness is plain to see. Would that I could behold the subject in person.

You asked after my parents, and I shall satisfy your curiosity. My father was Mr George Darcy, an only child, much to my grandmother's disappointment. From her journals, I know she suffered several disappointments before carrying my father to term. How grateful I am for her success, for without it, I would not be here.

As the heir, my grandparents trained my father to manage Pemberley from a very young age. Though he was merely a gentleman, albeit one of means, he secured the hand of my mother, Lady Anne Darcy, the second daughter of the late Earl of Matlock. My mother was delicate in health, but she possessed an unyielding spirit and was a kind mistress, always fair to those around her. I never heard her speak a harsh word to anyone, even a servant.

My mother suffered the loss of children, as my grandmother did. She was very fortunate to survive her confinement with Georgiana. My father doted on her, and when she passed, he lost a part of himself. I do not believe he ever fully recovered. Their marriage was a love match, something rare for those of my station. I do not know if their relationship began that way, but it certainly became so with time.

Lately, I have been reflecting on my own expectations for marriage. Not long ago, I believed I would follow the tradition of securing an advantageous match, but in recent months, my views on matrimony have shifted. Six months ago, I did not believe love was a possibility. I now entertain the notion of setting aside my family's expectations and pursuing happiness on my own terms. I am beginning to see that a marriage based on love is worth far more than one grounded in wealth or social standing.

But on to the more tantalising subject of Mr Blandishman. You have piqued my curiosity. What sort of gentleman is he, and what is his situation? Is he worthy of you? Are you entertaining his attentions? I trust your family approves—or have you, wisely, kept this gentleman a secret from your mother? I imagine Mrs Bennet would flood you with letters, eager to see you well-settled. You must tell me more of this man.

I thank you for sharing your aunt's maiden name—Partridge. There were two such families in Lambton. One remains within the vicinity of the village, whilst the other moved away fifteen years ago or so. Your aunt must be Madeline Partridge, the daughter of the former innkeeper at the Rose and Crown. I remember that Mr Partridge's health failed, and he left the inn to his brother and went to London in search of treatment. My father was told of his passing, but I heard nothing of his daughter.

Pray, tell me more of your aunt and uncle. Do they reside in the country or in Town? What is their situation? Perhaps Mr Gardiner is a landowner or prominent solicitor? I wish to know everything—about them and, of course, about you.

You asked when I must leave Ramsgate. I shall remain here with my sister until mid-September, after which we depart for London. There, I shall deliver Georgiana to my Aunt Matlock, where she will complete her education. She does not wish to return to school, and I have agreed, so I must also locate a suitable companion for her. We will remain in Town until the harvest is near and then go to Pemberley.

As I close this letter, I wish to tell you of an idea that has overtaken all my thoughts of late. It is rather bold, but I propose that we meet in person. I suspect our letters will cease to reach one another once I leave the Lake House. Therefore, I suggest we meet in April of 1813. This date allows ample time for my return to Ramsgate after the spring planting. For you, the wait will seem brief, but for me, separated by time, it will feel endless.

There is a tea shop in Ramsgate overlooking the sea. Its pastries and exotic teas are unmatched, and Mrs Peacock, the proprietor, exudes joy like no other. The shop is one of Ramsgate's hidden treasures, and I share its existence with you in confidence. Swear to keep it to yourself, lest unworthy souls descend upon my favourite spot and deprive me of Mrs Peacock's famous apple tarts before I can have my fill of them.

Whilst I do not yet understand what has kept me from the Lake House in your time, I promise that, if it is within my power, I shall be there to meet you on the day I mentioned above. Pray, say that you will agree.

I await your reply with eagerness.

Yours faithfully,

Fitzwilliam Darcy

Elizabeth slowly folded the letter and carefully placed it with her missives from the past. Meet? In person? The thought was entrancing.

She had never thought it possible, but now the prospect captivated her. The desire to meet Mr Darcy was undeniable, and she knew without hesitation that she would agree.

Mr Darcy's remarks regarding Mr Blandishman made her laugh as she read, and his insight into her mother's nature was uncannily accurate. He perfectly understood Mrs Bennet's eagerness for her daughters to marry well, and Elizabeth had indeed kept Mr Blandishman's interest from her mother for the precise reasons he had surmised.

Wasting no time, she sat down to write her reply.

Chapter Eleven

August 9, 1810
The Lake House
Ramsgate
Darcy

Waiting for a reply from Miss Bennet—*Elizabeth*—was interminable. Pretending she was now anything but 'Elizabeth' to him tested Darcy's patience in a way few other things did. There was no discernible pattern as to how long letters took to pass from 1810 to 1812, though it seemed to vary depending on the writer. From the dates on many of Elizabeth's replies, Darcy gathered that sometimes as little as a day passed before his letters traversed time to its destination.

His preoccupation had become apparent to Georgiana, and he had caught the speculative looks she cast his way. Oh, if only he could confide in her! But such a tale was beyond belief, and he could not expect her to accept it. Her current disillusionment with the superficial young ladies of society would surely increase her suspicions.

There was nothing for it—he must immerse himself in his work and the care of Georgiana, lest his thoughts drive him mad. At last, four days after sending his last letter, another arrived.

August 8, 1812

Dear Sir,

Pray forgive the delay in my reply. How absurd that sounds, when regular post would take far longer to arrive than our letters do. I began crafting my response as soon as I received your letter, but a number of tasks and troubles kept me from completing it until now.

Your flattering words regarding my appearance, sir, have touched me, though I must inform you that, according to my mother, I am only the fourth most beautiful Bennet daughter. Jane holds the highest place in her esteem. My sister Lydia follows next, being the liveliest and most like Mama herself. Kitty naturally follows, for she mirrors Lydia's behaviour as she seeks Mama's approval. I am deemed tolerable. Mama says that I am too brown from being in the sun and that my lack of ladylike accomplishments will deter many suitors. However, she considers poor Mary the least attractive of the Bennet girls—not to say that she is plain, but merely unremarkable by comparison.

Nevertheless, your kind words soothed my soul and give me hope that I may yet prove tolerable enough to tempt a gentleman into matrimony.

Your parents sound truly wonderful. I have often wished that mine shared such affection as yours did. I have spoken of Mr and Mrs Bennet before, so I shall not revisit those sentiments. How fortunate you are to have grown up surrounded by such felicity. It seems odd to me that, having witnessed the happiness of your parents, you would ever consider marrying for anything less. Yet, such is the way of the first circles.

Your father's death must have placed a heavy burden upon your shoulders. From our earlier letters, I have surmised that you were very young when you lost him. My father did not inherit Longbourn until he was three-and-thirty, which was after I was born. I do not think he would have proven as adept at managing Longbourn had he assumed control of the estate before gaining his majority. As it is, he shows little interest in its management, and I cannot imagine that would have changed had he inherited at a younger age.

I cannot fathom the pain your mother and grandmother must have endured since I am not married, and my mama had no such troubles. Five daughters in less than eight years! If only she had borne a son, her happiness would have been complete. Your early years must have been terribly lonely until your sister arrived. I am glad, for your sake, that you have her with you.

What caused your marital perspectives to change, if I may ask? Mine have always been steadfast, shaped by the turbulent family in which I was raised. I was sixteen before I fully grasped that my father's words to my mother held more than simple meaning, and older still before I understood the sharpness of his remarks. Mama's fretting was once less pronounced, but my father's continual belittling has done nothing to ease the situation. Perhaps her nerves might improve if he would guide her as a husband ought, rather than leaving her to flounder alone.

My mother is, I believe, content with her lot. Her status was elevated upon marrying my father. Although she is the great-granddaughter of a landed gentleman, her family has long since fallen from the ranks of the gentry. Her father, my Grandfather Gardiner, was a prominent solicitor in Meryton, and upon his passing, his business was willed to my uncle, Mr Andrew Phillips, who is married to my mother's sister, Harriet. Mother's brother, Mr Edward Gardiner, resides in London with his wife, the former Madeline Partridge.

The Gardiners live on Gracechurch Street near Cheapside, within sight of my uncle's warehouses. He owns a successful import and export business, and I suspect he earns more per annum than my father does from his estate.

Despise me if you dare, Mr Darcy, for my connexions. Though not as elevated as your own, my relations are dear to me. I hold deep affection for my Aunt and Uncle Gardiner. As I have mentioned, it is through their tender care that Jane and I have not become as wild as my younger sisters. From the age of thirteen, we spent several months each year in London under their guidance. Aunt Gardiner's instruction taught Jane and me the proper way to behave, and her influence is evident to all who know us.

I recall one such venture into town. It was in October of 1810, and I was nine-and-ten. My aunt had promised to give me a taste of London society. Jane accompanied me, and we eagerly anticipated spending the Little Season attending balls, soirees, and parties every night. That time is so memorable because, whilst we were in town, we heard that King George III had been officially declared insane, and his son, the Prince Regent, would assume control of the kingdom. But I digress.

After only a short time attending events, I found myself weary of the constant revelry. My aunt eyed me knowingly when I confessed this; whilst I do enjoy society, too much of it leaves me longing for peace and quiet. Thus, she took me to Hatchard's to choose a book. I was in search of a specific volume for myself and another for my father's birthday. I had but little time to find the ideal present, as his birthday was just three days away.

My dear aunt kindly spared time from her busy day to escort me about Town. She waited patiently as I browsed the volumes and did not so much as bat an eye when an unknown gentleman assisted me in selecting the perfect gift. She did, however, remind me of proper decorum on our return in the carriage! I shall forever be grateful for her gentle guidance—so different from Mama's scolding or Papa's indifference.

I know not if this memory conveys how dear my relations are to me, but there you have it. Now, on to Mr Blandishman, though I cannot agree that he is tantalising!

You are correct—Mama knows nothing of him. I made Jane swear to keep his visits a secret. I am not certain if one would call his attentions courting, precisely, though he calls on my brother twice a week.

Mr Blandishman is… unremarkable. He is of average height and build, with sandy brown hair and brown eyes. His mannerisms remind me of our favourite parson in Kent, though he lacks some of my cousin's more intolerable traits. His situation is favourable for a woman in my position, and should he offer a proposal, it would be folly to refuse him. You know well how Mr Collins fared, however, and can likely guess what course I shall take if I find that I cannot love him.

I wish you success in your search for a companion for your sister. Were I in your place, I would send inquiries ahead, so that when you arrive in town, you have prospective ladies ready for consideration. The position of a lady's companion is a coveted one, and such a woman holds great influence over her charge. She may either assist or hinder Miss Darcy's introduction to society, so only the most suitable candidate will do, especially when it comes to facing the harpies of the ton.

Regarding your proposed meeting, I shall make a note of it in my journal. Tomorrow, I intend to venture out in search of this magnificent establishment you described, for I absolutely refuse to wait until next spring to sample the pastries and teas you so highly recommend.

Mr Darcy, since writing the above, I have attended a dinner with my brother and sister and have learned something that may interest you.

We dined at the home of Mr and Mrs Nelson, a young and cheerful couple my brother-in-law has recently befriended. They have only lived in Ramsgate for six months or so. Mrs Nelson would get along famously with my mother, for she delights in gossiping about everyone and everything.

Tonight's topic of discussion was, surprisingly enough, the Lake House. Mrs Nelson claims to have it on good authority that the house has stood empty since last summer, though it has remained fully staffed. She expressed surprise that Jane would wish to stay in a house so marked by tragedy. When I pressed her for details, she admitted she knew little—only that something occurred last summer which drove the owners from Ramsgate, never to return.

Her account was rather dramatic, but if there is any truth in her words, something did indeed happen last year—next year for you—that will lead you to lease the house this year, in 1812. I shall keep my ears open for more information, though it seems the family kept the entire affair quiet, and no one truly knows what transpired.

Goodbye for now, Mr Darcy. I look forward to your next letter.

Yours,

E. Bennet

Darcy waited for the usual feelings of disgust and aversion to arise at the news of Elizabeth's connexions, but none came. Had his opinions shifted so significantly that the thought of a tradesman for an uncle no longer troubled him? Even more surprising was the jealousy that surged within him as he read of Mr Blandishman—so strong, in fact, that it had caused him to wrinkle her letter. That gentleman was all... *wrong* for her. He would have to tell her so. She claimed there was no understanding, no courtship, but why else would the man persist in calling at the Lake House if not to see Elizabeth? He could not believe it was *only* her brother that drew him there.

Yet what intrigued him most was her signature. *How I wish you were mine,* he thought, retrieving her likeness from his coat pocket—it was there most days now, for he could not bear to part with it even for a moment. He gazed at her face once more, a soft smile forming on his lips.

His thoughts returned to her letter. She had agreed to meet him! Now came the waiting. It would be difficult, but he would endure it. Her letter had sparked another idea; another opportunity to see her in person. He would be unable to do more than observe her from afar, but it was something.

As for the tittle-tattle this Mrs Nelson had related… what could have possibly happened? Surely, if the Darcy family had been involved in any tragedy, the gossips would have widely talked of it in Ramsgate and in Town. Why was there so little information? Darcy considered asking Elizabeth to enquire further, but her source seemed to have reached the limits of her knowledge. It was of no matter. Darcy would simply prepare for the worst and prevent it from happening—or, at the very least, he would be vigilant, for he had no way of knowing exactly what this 'tragedy' could entail.

For now, he was content. Elizabeth's letter had given him enough to ease his mind, and he was better able to focus on his work and on Georgiana. His sister brightened considerably after they spent a day together, and Darcy resolved to give her more attention during their remaining weeks in Ramsgate. He must temper his desire to communicate with Elizabeth; his lack of self-control should not cause Georgiana to suffer. There was nothing he could do to hasten the arrival of letters, and he would have to be satisfied to receive them whenever they came.

His commitment to Georgiana delayed his reply to Elizabeth's letter by several days. Thus, it was mid-August before he sanded, sealed, and placed his response on the salver.

Chapter Twelve

August 16, 1812
The Lake House
Ramsgate
Elizabeth

Nearly a week had passed, and still Elizabeth had not received another letter from Mr Darcy. Her previous notions about his arrogance and conceit began to resurface, teasing her thoughts as she invented all manner of explanations for the delay. Yet none seemed plausible, and she fretted that perhaps the gentleman had decided to sever their correspondence due to her plethora of *less-than-ideal* relations.

Jane noticed her disquiet and attributed it to Elizabeth's extended time indoors. Charles had insisted that his wife rest and regain her strength after she had suffered a brief spell of nausea earlier in the week. Though they had traced the cause to something she ate, and her symptoms soon abated, Elizabeth had dutifully kept her sister company.

"Lizzy, that is the third time you have sighed so dramatically," Jane teased as the sisters worked on yet another baby gown. "Are you thinking of a certain gentleman of our acquaintance?"

Elizabeth nearly laughed aloud. A gentleman *indeed* occupied her thoughts, though not one Jane—or she, for that matter—had ever met. "I assure you, my thoughts are far more agreeably engaged," she replied lightly.

"What could be more agreeable than contemplating a gentleman who pays you such tenacious attention?" Jane's tone was genuinely perplexed, and she glanced up from her work with a look of confusion.

"A gentleman paying me attention whom I *esteemed* would be a start," Elizabeth muttered. "Besides, I have told you, there is no formal understanding between Mr Blandishman and me."

"You do not esteem Mr Blandishman?"

Elizabeth pursed her lips and set aside her work before turning to her sister. "Mr Blandishman is a perfectly suitable man, but he possesses a streak of self-conceit that I find rather unappealing. His company is not entirely objectionable, yet I do not seek it. I neither dream of him nor look forward to our next conversation, even as he departs. He does not make my heart beat faster or cause my breath to quicken. Were I to compare my feelings for him to those of another acquaintance, I should place him somewhere between Sir William Lucas and Arnold Goulding."

Jane tut-tutted. "That is a poor assessment!" she said dejectedly. "I had so hoped you would form an attachment, so that I might tell Mama I succeeded where she did not."

Elizabeth laughed good-naturedly. "That is quite wicked, Jane! I applaud your deviousness. Alas, Mr Blandishman has yet to stir any passion within me. I made it clear that whilst his acquaintance is acceptable, we are *not* courting. He appears to accept that."

"Very well, Lizzy. I shall refrain from teasing you further on the matter. If you do not feel a passionate regard for him, then he is not the one for you." Jane smiled pleasantly, though Elizabeth thought she detected a trace of disappointment in her sister's eyes.

No, Elizabeth's *passions* lay elsewhere, but how could she explain to Jane that she had fallen in love with a figure from the past? The conversation lapsed into silence once more as they worked steadily for another half hour.

"Perhaps a walk would do you good," Jane suggested at length. "You have been tapping your foot madly for at least ten minutes. Go on. I can manage here, and I daresay Charles will return shortly to keep me company."

The speed with which Elizabeth set aside the gown caused Jane to raise an eyebrow. Thankfully, her sister said nothing. "I shall return in time for tea," Elizabeth promised, hurrying from the room.

"Take a footman!" Jane called after her. Elizabeth waved in acknowledgement as she made her way to prepare.

James, rather than John, attended her, maintaining a respectful distance as Elizabeth briskly walked towards the park. Her thoughts were in turmoil, shifting from concern that Mr Darcy had discarded her, to righteous anger at the possibility he could be so shallow. Her breath quickened, and her pace increased until she was nearly running. Rounding a corner near the fountain, she collided with a man in the path. The force of the collision sent them both sprawling. James caught her in time to prevent her from falling to the ground, but the man she had run into was not so fortunate and he now lay in a heap on the path.

She groaned inwardly as she realised it was Mr Blandishman. Trust that gentleman to be unable to keep his feet. Her more contrary thoughts chastised her—was he truly so terrible? He was here, after all, and not two years in the past. He had shown her attention, and she need not wait for delayed letters to feel his approbation.

"Oh, my dear Mr Blandishman!" she said impulsively, moving to his side and crouching down. "Are you well? I am terribly sorry. I was not attending as I walked."

"Have a care, Miss Bennet!" Mr Blandishman admonished, ignoring her outstretched hand as he got to his feet, brushing off his breeches and jacket. "This is a new coat, you know, and I should hate for it to be ruined by an inattentive young lady."

She drew closer to him and brushed some dry grass from the front of the coat. "Forgive me?" she asked, infusing her voice with a forced chagrin and apology. She lowered her gaze, as she had often seen Lydia do. "I fear my mind has been a jumble today. I was quite lost in my thoughts."

Mr Blandishman stilled, his attention shifting from his attire to her. There was a gleam of speculation in his eyes, and Elizabeth felt a flush rise to her cheeks. She knew exactly where his thoughts were leading, and in his arrogance, he would surely assume he was the cause of her inner turmoil.

"Dare I ask if *I* am the subject of these 'jumbled thoughts'?" he enquired, his voice laced with smugness.

She was correct—he believed she referred to him. But a tiny, wicked voice whispered in her mind. *Did you not intend for him to think that? Is that not why you acted so?* Yes. She had wanted to punish Mr Darcy, even as she acknowledged the futility of it; he was not here, and it was she alone who would suffer for offering Mr Blandishman encouragement she did not mean. Instant regret for her impulsive actions consumed her. *Dear heavens, did I just mimic Lydia?*

Elizabeth stepped back, leaving a proper distance between them. "I am not at liberty to share my thoughts at this time," she murmured softly, her cheeks burning with embarrassment. The fear of what her actions might provoke gnawed at her. Mr Blandishman would assume she wished to increase his affection through suspense and would pursue her with even more determination.

He smiled knowingly. "I am a patient man," he told her, offering his arm. "You will confide in time. I look forward to the day you do."

Elizabeth accepted his offered arm gingerly, as though it were a snake that might bite. Mr Blandishman led her around the walking paths towards the fountain, regaling her with a stream of nonsensical thoughts and ideas. He required no response, leaving Elizabeth's mind to wander towards to more pleasant matters.

They parted ways a quarter of an hour later, James still keeping a respectful distance as Elizabeth made her way back to the Lake House. Tea would be served soon, and all she wished for now was solitude.

"Letters for you, miss," Susan greeted Elizabeth as she entered her chamber. "I've left them on your dressing table."

"Thank you, Susan." She had been expecting a letter from Charlotte, and perhaps it had finally arrived. A vain hope stirred within her that a letter from Mr Darcy might also be amongst the stack, but disappointment awaited her. The second missive was from her mother.

All the usual fiddle-faddle and enquiries about Elizabeth's progress in securing a husband filled the letter. Charlotte's, however, proved far more enjoyable, and Elizabeth began composing a reply to her friend before tea.

That evening's engagement drew them from the Lake House to a soiree hosted by one of Charles's new acquaintances. Mr Tobias Smith and his wife, Isabelle, had a residence just a few streets away. Mr Smith was involved in trade, but such matters had never concerned Charles, nor did they trouble his wife or sister.

The party was lavish and loud, the rooms of the house filled to bursting, and by the time Elizabeth found her bed, it was the early hours of the morning. She fell into an exhausted slumber and dreamed of Mr Darcy.

Her low spirits lingered the next day, and she half-heartedly played the pianoforte after breakfast before curling up in a chair with a book. Smythe brought her the post since Jane was still abed, and she eagerly sorted through the stack. There, at the very bottom of the pile, was a letter from Mr Darcy. Her heart rejoiced—he had not forsaken her! The rest of the post forgotten, Elizabeth took her letter to her chambers so as not to be disturbed.

August 16, 1810

Dear Elizabeth,
I must apologise for my delayed reply. It has been a busy week. Georgiana has suffered some neglect from me, so consumed have I been in business, and thus I dedicated much of the past several days to her entertainment. We visited the shops and Mrs Peacock's tea parlour. Have you gone yet, and tasted her pastries?

Amongst other matters, I have sent numerous enquiries in search of a companion for my sister. I have received several favourable replies and hope to interview candidates immediately upon my return to London...

Mr Darcy wrote about the trivialities of day-to-day life, captivating Elizabeth's attention and drawing her into every detail. With each word, she came to know him better and lost a little more of her heart to him. She reflected on her pique from the day before with regret. Not only had she given Mr Blandishman hope when there was none, but she had once again judged Mr Darcy too hastily.

He responded to her news about the King's impending declaration of insanity, though he seemed to overlook her revelations from Mrs Nelson. His impressions of her Aunt and Uncle Gardiner were also favourable, leaving her with fresh guilt for having prematurely condemned him.

His thoughts on Mr Blandishman were particularly diverting. *He sounds every bit as colourless as his name,* Mr Darcy wrote. *Has there ever been an appellation that suited a man so well? Would you truly be happy with such a gentleman?*

Elizabeth knew she would not. Mr Blandishman would make some woman a suitable husband, but it would not be her. Mayhap she could introduce him to Mary.

She and Mr Darcy continued exchanging letters through the remainder of August and into September. With each passing day, the time of Mr Darcy's departure from Ramsgate drew closer, and with each letter, Elizabeth fell deeper and deeper in love with the gentleman from Derbyshire. How she would miss him when he left!

Mr Blandishman had indeed taken Elizabeth's behaviour that fateful day as encouragement, despite her earlier words of disinterest, and he continued to call at least twice a week, sometimes more. Elizabeth began avoiding the house whenever he arrived. Nevertheless, Charles and Jane felt compelled to ask him to dine each week. With extra caution, Elizabeth maintained the strictest propriety in her unwanted suitor's company, enduring his increased attentions without complaint. It *was* her fault, after all.

One last letter arrived for Elizabeth the day Mr Darcy was to depart for London in 1810. She opened it slowly, knowing this would be the last she heard from him until his return to Ramsgate the following year.

September 15, 1810

My dearest Elizabeth,

I write with a heavy heart, knowing that we will be apart for some months. Your letters have become very dear to me, and I do not know how I shall manage without them. The amusing anecdotes and astute observations you share have delighted me beyond measure, and your intelligence has captivated my interest. Your wit and vivacity have enchanted me; I am under your spell. Even now, I search for some means by which I might shift my responsibilities to another and remain in Ramsgate through the winter.

There will be no chance for your reply before my departure this afternoon, and so this moment must serve to express the deepest sentiments of my heart. My love for you, Elizabeth Bennet of Longbourn, is undeniable. Though we have yet to meet in person, I know that day will come, and when it does, every sentiment written here shall be voiced without hesitation. It is not my place to plead for your hand, though it is my greatest desire. Instead, I ask only that you refrain from acting hastily during these months apart. Do not throw your future away on Mr Blandishman. You are my equal in every way, and to learn that your hand has been given to another would be unbearable.

I love you. Wait for me.

Enclosed is a token of my esteem. Think of me when you wear it, and may this talisman lessen the pain of our separation.

Sincerely yours,

Fitzwilliam Darcy

Enclosed in the letter was a beautiful silver chain. The links formed delicately crafted flowers, and Elizabeth loved the necklace instantly. Placing it around her neck, her fingers gently caressed the shining metal. He knew her so well.

I will wait, she promised him, though he could neither see nor hear her. *No matter how long it takes.*

Chapter Thirteen

September 23, 1810
Darcy House
London
Darcy

Darcy made the journey to London in good time and soon settled into his study, immersing himself in business matters. Letters from his steward spoke of the harvest and the preparations underway to see it through. His Aunt Tilda wasted no time in sending a summons—could it be called anything less? Darcy had agreed to dine with them in two days' time. Georgiana would also attend, as it was to be a small, family-only affair.

A letter from his cousin Richard awaited his attention. The colonel would be in London on leave in a few days and requested a room at Darcy House during his stay. *Mother is determined to have me married off before I must return to my regiment,* Richard had written. *I will not have it, and so I must throw myself upon your mercy.* Darcy was always glad to host Richard and wasted no time in penning a reply.

Charles Bingley had also written, asking Darcy to join him at their club for luncheon the next week. Or was it this week? Bingley had terribly blotted the date, and Darcy sighed as he attempted to decipher his friend's atrocious penmanship. He would have to send a note to Bingley asking for clarification.

Another less welcome letter sat amongst the stack. Lady Catherine had written, demanding that Darcy spend Christmas in Kent to finalise wedding plans for him and her daughter. He set it aside, knowing his reply would require careful handling, lest Lady Catherine descend upon London to berate him in person.

Despite all that demanded his attention, Darcy's thoughts lingered on Elizabeth. He wondered what she was doing in Ramsgate and dearly wished he could write to her to enquire. He briefly considered sending a man to Ramsgate bearing a letter, but quickly discarded the idea. They would think him mad! Besides, he had no way of knowing whether the letter would traverse time if he was not in residence.

Everywhere he looked, he saw Elizabeth's image—at his dinner table, in the library, seated at his pianoforte... The thoughts were constant, and despite his best efforts, he could not banish them entirely. Richard's timely arrival proved a welcome distraction.

"Hello, Cousin!" the colonel cried, barging into his study without being announced. "Why the long face? Has the dog died?"

"I do not have a dog, Rich," Darcy chuckled. "No, it is merely business concerns which occasion my scowl. Tell me, how long shall I have the pleasure of your company?"

"Six weeks, mayhap a little longer." Richard shrugged. "There is talk of a change in command. They may reassign me to the continent. Have you heard? The Little Coriscan's reach spreads."

Darcy grimaced. He had heard the news months before Richard. "Yes, I have heard of it," he said. "Is the Foreign Office concerned about Napoleon's continued campaign to control all of Europe?"

"They do not believe the little Frenchman poses much of a threat—at least not to our mainland," Richard answered slowly.

"I gather that you disagree?"

Richard nodded, fiddling with his cufflinks. "He has annexed Holland and Westphalia. Such men are never content with a little war. No, they must expand their empires to the farthest reaches of the Earth and beyond."

"Much like our own empire," Darcy mused.

"Our troops *are* spread rather thin," Richard agreed. "Mark my words, they will begin bolstering the militias and calling for new recruits to the Regulars before long."

"You would know better than I, and so I bow to your judgement." Darcy pulled a stack of letters from the corner of his desk. "On another matter, I have narrowed down the list of candidates for Georgiana's companion."

"She is not to return to school?" Richard looked baffled.

"Did I not write of it?" Darcy recounted his sister's circumstances, and Richard agreed with his decision to keep her home.

"Tell me of your candidates."

"The first is Arabella Frost," Darcy said immediately. "I have her letters of reference, but further enquiries suggest she is as cold as her name implies."

"Georgiana would wilt under such a creature," Richard agreed.

"The second is more favourable. Her name is Martha Stewart. By all accounts, she is matronly and warm. Her accomplishments are not what I would hope; she lacks experience with languages and the pianoforte, but I believe she would be agreeable for our girl."

"And the last?"

"Agatha Younge. She is a young widow, and her references are impeccable. She has aided the daughters of earls and baronets in their come outs in recent years. Her knowledge of French, Italian, and Spanish is extensive; she is a gifted musician; and she is younger than most, which would suit Georgie well. Whilst I desire a companion to guide her, I also wish for Georgiana to view the lady as a friend."

Richard nodded. "I propose we interview Mrs Younge and Mrs Stewart. One of them will surely suit."

"Agreed," Darcy replied. "I shall instruct my man to send note at once."

"I will take myself off to my room until dinner," Richard replied. "My usual suite?"

Darcy nodded absently, already focused on future interviews with candidates. His cousin saw himself out.

Within a week, Darcy hired Mrs Younge as Georgiana's companion. With her employment, his sister no longer required his attention for several hours each day. The extra time was both a blessing and a curse. He managed his affairs with far greater efficiency, but it left him with too much time to brood.

Richard was quick to notice his preoccupation. "What ails you, cousin?" he asked one evening as they enjoyed a glass of port. "You are in a brown study, and I do not know what to make of it. I have never seen you so distracted."

Darcy shrugged. Was he to tell his cousin that he was in love with a woman he had never met, let alone one who lived two years in the future? "It is nothing," he dissembled.

"If it is nothing, I shall eat my hat! Who is she? Some fair-faced girl just out of the schoolroom? A buxom country lass?"

"What makes you think it is a lady?"

Richard scoffed. "An actress then? Or the milkmaid!"

Darcy scowled. "That is not what I meant. How can you speculate that my preoccupation is due to a woman? Could it not be estate matters? Investments? The coming harvest?"

His cousin looked at him knowingly. "All these things you have faced before, and they have never rendered you a distracted fool. No, it is certainly a lady who has you so tangled up. Tell me about her. What is her name? What county does she call home?"

"I cannot say," Darcy stammered.

"Cannot or will not?" Richard countered.

"Cannot! It is a peculiar situation, and I do not know what to make of it."

Richard produced a flask from his coat and added some of the liquid to two empty glasses. "Then I shall ply you with drink until your tongue loosens," he chortled. "Come, Darcy. It would not do to waste Pater's French brandy. It is better than port, anyway."

"The earl will skin you alive for stealing his best," Darcy murmured, taking a sip.

Before long, the entire story had spilled out. Richard had surprisingly few questions for him and seemed to accept the entire tale with very little skepticism.

"There is only one thing for it," he said when Darcy concluded. "You must find a way to see her. Not in two years, but now."

"Am I to travel to Hertfordshire and throw myself at her feet? Oh, yes, that would be a fine idea."

"You said she has relations in Town. Investigate and see if you can encounter her. Or come to know the relations. They might throw her into your path."

A memory tickled Darcy's mind. "I have it!" he blurted. Opening a desk drawer, he retrieved Elizabeth's letters. After a moment of searching, he found it.

"Here." He thrust the letter at his cousin. "She is in London in October of this year! I could see her at Hatchard's."

"There is no date," Richard said, bewildered.

"I do not need one. There is enough information here to deduce that she will be in the shop during the last week of October. That is but three weeks away. I can watch for her."

Richard raised his brow. "So, you will skulk about the shop just waiting for her to appear?"

"I know what she looks like... roughly, at least. It could work, and it would not require me to appear in Meryton unannounced."

"Going to her home would certainly be easier, but if you meet her in the past, would you alter the course of her future?"

Darcy shrugged. "I do not know. This is as much a mystery to me as you."

"Start with Hatchard's, then. If you grow desperate, we can contrive some way for you to meet her." Richard downed his glass in one gulp.

Darcy was silent for a time before recalling something else his cousin ought to know. "Wickham came to the Lake House," he said softly.

Richard snorted. "What did that reprobate want this time?"

"He wished for me to bestow the Kympton living upon him when Mr Graham retires."

"The gall of the man!" Richard laughed uproariously. "You turned him down, I hope?"

"I did. He has vowed revenge."

"How frightening. Are you shaking in your boots?" Richard poured himself more brandy and held the glass without taking a drink.

"Wickham is harmless. He speaks of grand plans but lacks the ambition or means to carry out his threats." Darcy gathered Elizabeth's letters and returned them to their place. "I am not concerned about him. Now, I must retire. I have meetings with my solicitor in the morning."

"Goodnight, Cousin," Richard said before yawning widely. "I shall not be long behind you."

"Do me a favour and save some of the brandy for tomorrow."

The weeks of October passed in a haze and before Darcy knew it, the last week of the month had arrived. He began visiting Hatchard's, spending hours there. He would choose a book and settle into a chair in the corner where he could watch the door. At the end of each day, he would purchase a stack of books to please the proprietor, who, in return, let him be.

On the third day, *she* came. The bell to the shop jingled as the door opened, and Darcy glanced up from the tome in his hand, fully expecting the new arrival to be anyone but Elizabeth. Yet there she was, a vision before him. Her likeness had not prepared him for the true beauty of *his* lady. She hid her hair under a fashionable bonnet, save for the dark and lustrous curls that framed her lovely face and teased her alluring neck. She was smiling at something her companion had said, which caused her eyes to sparkle.

Her eyes are very fine! Darcy thought. He glanced at her companion and recognised an older version of Miss Madeline Partridge—Mrs Gardiner, Elizabeth's aunt.

"I will not be long," Elizabeth assured the lady. Her voice was melodic, warm, and rich. Darcy was entranced.

"You always say that when we come to Hatchard's and yet we invariably spend an hour here." Mrs Gardiner laughed, with no hint of censure in her tone.

Darcy watched Elizabeth move towards the back of the shop. He rose slowly, tucking the book he had been reading under his arm, and with measured steps, followed her to the same row of shelves. He watched her discreetly as she examined one volume after another, discarding each.

"Ah ha!" she exclaimed softly, as her eyes alighted on a book gracing the top shelf. Stretching up on her toes, she still fell short by several inches. She was quite petite; Darcy easily towered over her.

"May I be of assistance?" he asked quietly but startling her just the same.

"Oh, would you, sir?" she asked, her expression hopeful and grateful. "It is that book on botany there. My father has the other two volumes. We have been searching for this one for months!"

"I have the entire collection myself," Darcy replied, stepping closer. His gaze fixed on her countenance, he drank in her vibrancy, committing every detail to memory. Without looking away, he reached up and retrieved the book. Slowly, he lowered his arm and held it out to her.

Elizabeth's cheeks turned a delightful shade of pink as she took the volume gingerly. "I thank you, sir," she whispered before turning to flee down the row.

"Anything for you, Elizabeth." He spoke, but she did not hear him.

Far from satisfying his need, seeing Elizabeth only heightened his desire to be with her once more. Business soon pulled him away from London, preventing him from impulsively going to Hertfordshire. He was more in love with her than ever! How he would survive the coming months was beyond his understanding.

Chapter Fourteen

November 24, 1812-February 14, 1813
The Lake House
Ramsgate
Elizabeth

In the two months since Darcy's last letter, Elizabeth had done her best to maintain her equanimity, but it was proving more and more difficult with each passing day. She missed him, and she was not afraid to admit it. Despite knowing full well that she could not send him a letter for months, she penned a few lines for him every day, creating a journal of her comings and goings.

There was little to tell. Mr Blandishman continued his visits, and Elizabeth often found it difficult to keep a civil tongue. The more she came to know him, the more his presence displeased her. He was both obtuse and oblivious. Any other gentleman might have recognised her lukewarm responses to his inane conversation as a lack of interest, but not Mr Blandishman. Her reticence only seemed to encourage him, even after she reminded him that she did not desire a formal courtship. She remained at a loss as to how she might dissuade him without appearing rude.

Jane's labour began early on the morning of the twenty-fourth of November. The Bingleys sent for the midwife, but she was already attending another birth and only arrived after several hours, assistant in tow.

"You've some time yet, madam," Mrs Taylor, the midwife, told Jane. Elizabeth stood at a respectable distance. She knew it was not entirely proper for her to be in the room, but Jane had begged her to remain, and she could not refuse her most beloved sister.

Hours passed, and by the next morning, Jane had made little progress. Mrs Taylor was quick to reassure them.

"'Tis the first birth, ma'am. The labour usually progresses slowly." Mrs Taylor then left after being summoned to another's bedside. By the time she returned, night had fallen once more, and Jane was utterly exhausted. She lay in bed, her hair damp with perspiration, her breathing shallow. Elizabeth sat beside her, holding her hand and whispering words of comfort.

"I cannot do it, Lizzy," Jane whispered. "I thought I could, but I cannot. The pain is too much!"

The midwife remained oddly quiet as she examined her patient. Elizabeth did not like the concerned look on the woman's face. Mrs Taylor furrowed her brow and creased her forehead in concentration.

"What is it?" Elizabeth asked her.

Mrs Taylor stepped away from the bed and gestured for Elizabeth to follow. "Your sister is bleeding heavily," she murmured softly. "If the babe does not come soon, I fear for her life...as well as the child's."

Elizabeth's blood ran cold. "No," she breathed. "Jane cannot die!"

"Best be praying for a miracle, then," Mrs Taylor replied. "She's in a bad way. I've no doubt she'll have no more after this one. I've seen the like before."

Elizabeth nodded solemnly, immediately beginning silent prayers. Jane moaned as another wave of pain wracked her frame. Already weakened by her prolonged illness, it now seemed she might not have the strength to endure this painful trial.

Around midnight, Jane seemed to find some hidden reserve of strength. She rallied, and when the midwife checked her progress, her expression was finally one of satisfaction.

"It will be time to push soon," she said cheerfully. "You will hold your wee babe in less than an hour, Mrs Bingley."

Jane cried out as another pain gripped her. When it subsided, a determined gleam lit her eyes. Thirty minutes later, Mrs Taylor declared her ready to push.

"Let us move you to the birthing chair, madam," she said. With Elizabeth on one side and the midwife on the other, they guided Jane to the chair and helped her settle. Ten minutes later, Mrs Taylor placed a swaddled, tawny-haired boy into his aunt's arms.

"'Tis just a little longer, and we can get you to bed," Mrs Taylor said, patting Jane's arm soothingly. Jane's only response was another cry of pain. The joyous expression on the midwife's face turned to concern, and she moved swiftly to check her patient once more.

"Hand the lad to the maid, Miss Bennet!" she barked. "There's another."

Another? Another baby? Despite her shock, Elizabeth immediately followed the midwife's directions. She prepared another swaddling cloth and waited anxiously by Mrs Taylor's side.

"Now, Mrs Bingley! Push!"

Jane did so, and a moment later, the cry of another infant filled the room.

"'Tis a wee girl," Mrs Taylor said. "Well done, Mrs Bingley. 'Tis a rare thing to have twins, and rarer still they be a boy and a girl!" She handed Elizabeth the squalling babe who was now wrapped in clean linen, having used the swaddling cloth to wipe her clean. Sally stood nearby with Jane's son in her arms.

"Go show Mr Bingley his children whilst I help Mrs Bingley to bed," Mrs Taylor directed. "My assistant will aid me."

Sally followed Elizabeth from the room and they nearly collided with Charles in the hallway. Her brother looked dreadful—his eyes bloodshot, and his hair a matted mess. He had long since discarded his coat and his cravat, and his rumpled white lawn shirt was beyond repair.

"Is Jane...?" he trailed off, the concern and anticipation on his face breaking Elizabeth's heart.

"Jane is resting. It was a hard labour. But see here! You have a son... and a daughter." Elizabeth smiled broadly as she and Sally presented her niece and nephew to their father.

"Twins!" Charles stared at the babies in amazement. "May I hold them?"

"Certainly," Elizabeth chuckled. "Which will you hold first? Jane is not ready to see you yet."

"I... might I hold my son?" Sally stepped forward and handed the tiny boy to his father. Charles's eyes shone with tears, the love on his face a sight to behold.

"Hello, William," Charles whispered. "Welcome to the world. You and your sister have given us all quite a trial!"

"What will you name your daughter?" Elizabeth asked.

"Margaret Elizabeth," he said softly, "for my mother and my sister."

Elizabeth's heart warmed, and she drew the little bundle in her arms closer. "I hope for your sake she takes more after her mama than her aunt," she teased gently. She wondered briefly for whom her nephew had been named, but Charles was already speaking again.

"I would have no cause to repine if she took after you," Charles argued.

The door to the bedchamber opened. "Mrs Bingley is ready to see you now, sir," Mrs Taylor said. "My work here is done. I'll be going, but will return tomorrow to check on your wife. She needs rest, sir. Her ordeal was no easy matter."

If only he realised... Elizabeth thought, but said nothing. Charles need not know how worried the midwife had been for Jane.

Now propped up on a pile of pillows, Jane blinked sleepily as Charles and Elizabeth entered the room.

"It was not a dream, then?" she asked. "There are two?"

"There are two," Charles confirmed. "Meet William Charles and Margaret Elizabeth. They are as beautiful as their mother."

Elizabeth placed her niece in Jane's arms as Charles sat beside his wife, holding their son. Their heads bent together as they admired the precious bundles they held. Elizabeth suddenly felt superfluous and retreated quietly from the room. The Bingleys did not lift their gaze from their children as she closed the door behind her.

Sally was waiting for her.

"Did you summon the wet nurse?" Elizabeth asked. "I believe your mistress will need her services sooner rather than later."

"Yes, miss—half an hour ago," Sally confirmed. "The nursery and her chamber are ready and waiting."

"You are a treasure," Elizabeth said gratefully. "I imagine my sister will be ready to sleep shortly. There is a cradle in Mrs Bingley's room for one child. Is there another in the house?"

"I shall check storage," Sally said. "The cradle in the mistress's chamber belonged to the master. The owner of the house may have stored another in the attic."

Elizabeth nodded. "I must retire. I shall be of no use to my sister if I do not rest."

Despite barely having slept for two days, Elizabeth found she could not settle. Her nephew's name brought Mr Darcy to mind. True, his name was a little more formal—*Fitzwilliam*—but she could not help thinking of him as Charles named his son.

Only a few more months, Elizabeth told herself. *I can manage that.*

Elizabeth dispatched letters to family announcing the birth of Master William Charles Bingley and Miss Margaret Elizabeth Bingley. She waxed poetic about the charms of the newest additions to the family, describing them in considerable detail to her father and her brother's sisters. Replies came swiftly, and Charles left her to read and reply to them, addressed to her or not. They ranged from ecstatic enthusiasm to lukewarm felicitations. The former was from Mrs Bennet, who called Jane a clever girl to give her husband an heir so soon. The latter was from Caroline Bingley, and her words were so insincere that Elizabeth chose not to share them with Charles or Jane. Neither needed Miss Bingley's poison to mar their felicity.

Jane's recovery was slow. The birth of her children had exhausted her, and whatever strength she had regained in recent months had vanished. She insisted on helping the wet nurse feed the babies. Although the woman assured her mistress she had enough milk for both babies, Jane wished to leave nothing to chance, and helped with the feedings herself throughout the day.

Elizabeth's routine returned to what it had been during Jane's illness in the early summer. She performed the duties of mistress and cared for her sister whilst lavishing attention on William and Margaret.

Mr Blandishman kept his distance for four weeks after Jane's confinement before calling at the Lake House once more. Elizabeth received him with barely concealed impatience, determined to keep the meeting short so she could assist Jane. *Perhaps I ought to have Smythe say I am not at home to callers,* she mused.

"Miss Bennet!" the gentleman cried as he entered the room. "It has been far too long since I had the pleasure of your company. Have you fared well? You must miss our strolls in the park. Might I tempt you away from the house for half an hour to enjoy such an activity?"

"I am sorry, but I must decline," she replied. "Jane has need of me, and I do not foresee that changing anytime soon."

"Could a maid not attend to your sister and her children?" Mr Blandishman whinged.

Elizabeth frowned. "I am here as a guest to my sister to assist her through her confinement and recovery," she reminded him. "I will not abandon my duties. My niece and nephew are still quite small and require attention, and I know Mrs Bingley would prefer that care to come from family rather than servants. I do hope you understand."

Mr Blandishman frowned briefly before offering an ingratiating smile. "Of course, of course. I quite understand. Your dedication to your loved ones is commendable, Miss Bennet. It is one of the many things I admire about you." He stepped closer and took Elizabeth's hand, raising it to his lips to place a kiss upon it. It was all she could do to keep from pulling away in disgust.

"Might I call again in a few days? I have missed you dreadfully."

She could not say the same. "Please remember, sir, that we are not courting, nor are we engaged. If you are content to a visit brief, I am amenable. Charles will enjoy speaking with you as well." Charles, she knew, could converse easily with nearly anyone, and Elizabeth would gladly share her visitor with him.

"Very good," came the slightly dejected reply. "I must be going now. Lots to do."

"Thank you for calling, sir." Elizabeth breathed a sigh of relief as Smythe showed him out. Hurrying upstairs to check on Jane, Mr Darcy's admonition not to waste herself on Mr Blandishman resounded in her thoughts.

As the weeks passed and her unwanted suitor continued to pay her a prodigious amount of attention, Elizabeth wondered if her friendship with Mr Darcy had forever altered her perception of other men. She had always valued intelligent conversation, yet part of her questioned whether she might have been more receptive to Mr Blandishman's overtures if she had never become acquainted with the enigmatic man from the past. It seemed a foolish notion, especially considering the similarities between Mr Blandishman and Mr Collins, for whom she had never entertained such thoughts.

As it stood, Elizabeth found herself constantly comparing one gentleman to the other whenever she was in Mr Blandishman's company, and her patience grew increasingly thin. His visits to the Lake House became an ordeal, and she endured them as best she could, always seeking to keep them brief. She refused to walk out with him more than once a week. Mr Blandishman, however, remained blissfully unaware, ascribing her reluctance to her devotion to her sister. Elizabeth could not help but wonder if he had ever truly heard her rejection, or, like Mr Collins, believed it only a matter of time before she accepted his proposal.

Though Elizabeth tried to disabuse Mr Blandishman of his assumptions, helping Jane became her ready excuse whenever she wished to avoid his company. Jane, in turn, never refused her sister's help, though she often cast knowing looks when Elizabeth suddenly reappeared at her side after only recently leaving it. Still, Jane did not press her, for which Elizabeth was most grateful, and she offered no explanation in return. There were only a few months remaining until she would meet Mr Darcy. After that, she could introduce Jane to the man she loved and forget Mr Blandishman forever.

But it was only February. Mr Darcy had promised to meet her in April. She would have to endure a little longer.

Chapter Fifteen

January 6, 1811
Pemberley
Derbyshire
Darcy

Darcy sat by Georgiana's bedside, reading aloud from one of her favourite novels. She lay back against the pillows, her eyes closed as she listened. Though she was on the mend now, the last week had been filled with worry. Georgiana had caught a cold just after Christmas, and it had swiftly worsened. Her sniffles had turned into deep, wet coughs that wracked her body as she struggled to breathe. Day after day, Darcy remained at her side as she battled the fever that seemed determined to claim her life. Finally, the night before, her fever had broken, and she had slept peacefully for the first time in days. Now, she half-listened to her brother's reading as her breathing gradually evened out. Her head relaxed into the pillow, and sleep overcame her.

"Get some rest, Master Fitzwilliam," Mrs Reynolds urged, placing a hand on his shoulder and patting it tenderly. The familiar gesture soothed him; he had known the loyal housekeeper since he was four years old, and he held her in high esteem. "Miss Darcy will still be here when you wake," she continued. "I'll keep an eye on her. It will do none of us any good if you fall ill too."

"Very well, Mrs Reynolds," Darcy replied, rising to his feet. "You always know best."

"That I do. Best that you never forget it," she replied, waggling a finger at him—but her smile and twinkling eyes softened her words with kindness. Taking her master's seat next to Georgiana's bed, she set down the workbasket she carried and began mending an article of clothing with practised hands.

Darcy left the room—his valet awaited him in his bedchamber, and after shedding his restrictive clothing, he collapsed into his bed, succumbing to an exhausted slumber. A pair of fine eyes and the light and pleasing figure of Elizabeth Bennet filled Darcy's dreams. Since seeing her at Hatchard's, his nighttime imaginings had taken on a life of their own. Where once his mind had filled the gaps of his knowledge of her, now it refined his memories, engraving her image upon his very soul. Each time he woke, he longed to return to that dreamy realm where he could hold Elizabeth in his arms.

Even now, worn through as he was, Darcy could not elude her. His sleep was restful, yet still dominated by thoughts of Elizabeth. When he awoke, he yearned for her once more, but dutifully rose to attend his ablutions. Georgiana remained his priority. His fear for her life had not entirely abated, and he was eager to see for himself that her health still improved.

Mrs Reynolds had been true to her word and had not left Georgiana's side all night. Darcy traded places with her, instructing his faithful housekeeper to seek her own bed for a few hours. When she made to demure, he gave her an imperious look, as though willing her to obey.

"None of that, Master," she chortled. "The Darcy stare never worked on me when your father did it, and it shan't work for you either. But never fear, I'll do as you say. Heaven knows I could use the rest. These old bones do not sit up all night as well as they once did."

"You are a treasure, Mrs Reynolds," Darcy told her. "Thank you for your care."

"I shall have a tray sent up if it pleases you," she said with a glare that commanded he accept.

Darcy grinned and nodded. Mrs Reynolds took her work basket and left, leaving Darcy alone with his sister.

Georgiana stirred, her eyes fluttering open. "Good morning, Fitzwilliam," she said hoarsely.

"Good morning, poppet." He brushed a lock of hair away from her eyes. "How are you feeling today?"

"My throat hurts, but that is all," she said. "The pain in my chest and the aches in my body are gone. How long was I…unaware?"

"It was nearly a se'ennight," Darcy answered, his throat tightening with emotion. "I am beyond relieved that you are awake now. Would you like something to eat? Mrs Reynolds is sending up a tray."

"I think some tea and toast would be agreeable."

Darcy smiled. "And perhaps some broth later?"

Georgiana nodded. "Yes, that sounds lovely. Will you read to me after breakfast?"

"I can for a while, but then I must see to some business. Lady Catherine has written, and I need to pen a reply."

"It displeased her we did not spend Christmas in Kent, did it not?" Georgiana smiled weakly. "I can only imagine how much angrier she would have been if I had fallen ill where Anne could have succumbed herself."

Darcy chuckled. "You have taken her measure well. She wishes me to attend her as usual in April, but I intend to decline. I plan to review her estate books in late February, so that we can go to the Lake House in March. You would benefit from the sea air, and your needs must always come before her wants." *And it would mean resuming his letters to Elizabeth that much sooner.*

"Your care for me is exemplary, brother. Thank you. Has Mrs Younge kept herself occupied?"

"She has. Your companion has gone to Lambton several times when the roads are clear enough, bringing back tisanes and tinctures. Her concern for you has been palpable. To know you are awake this morning will please her."

A maid entered with the breakfast tray and set it down upon a small table Darcy drew nearer to the bed. He helped his sister with her tea and toast, delighted that she was able to eat two whole slices.

"I am tired now," she said after finishing. "Go. My maid can see to me whilst you attend to your work. Mrs Younge can read to me if I awaken before you return."

"Very well." Darcy rose, bending to kiss his sister's forehead. "I love you, Georgie. Sleep well."

She was asleep before he reached the door.

Darcy's thoughts drifted to Elizabeth as he struggled to answer his letters of business. It had been a long four months since her last letter, and it would be at least another two before he could return to Ramsgate. Was she pining for him as he was for her? He selfishly hoped so. There would be much to share when he was finally at the Lake House. Had her sister come through her confinement well? Was the babe thriving? And how would she respond when she learned he had seen her at Hatchard's?

After completing his letters of business, he turned to Lady Catherine's missive. Drawing it towards him, he read it again.

December 27, 1810

Darcy,

I am most seriously displeased that you chose to remain in Derbyshire for the festive season. Anne missed your presence dreadfully and was morose the entire month of December. How could you be so unfeeling and cruel? Your father and mother were never so callous, and they would weep at your behaviour.

Since I did not have the pleasure of your company this winter, I expect you here in April. You will review my estate books and then we shall finalise the plans for you and Anne's wedding. She is nearing five-and-twenty, as you know, and you are not getting any younger either. You have had ample time to sow your wild oats, and now you must do your duty to your family. I shall not brook disappointment in this!

I shall have your usual rooms prepared and expect you no later than the tenth of April. I will not tolerate your refusal in this matter and will know how to act should you choose not to oblige me. Bring Georgiana with you. I must evaluate her progress in her education. A gentleman cannot possibly know what it takes to raise a young lady. You and Richard must be neglecting the finer details of her studies.

Write to me immediately.

Yours, etc.,

Lady Catherine de Bourgh

His aunt's signature was all flourishes and embellishments. Trust Aunt Catherine to use her courtesy title even when writing to her family. Drawing a fresh sheet of paper, he picked up his quill and began to compose his reply.

January 7, 1811

Dear Aunt Catherine,

I regret to inform you I cannot come to Rosings Park in April. Georgiana has been seriously ill, and my physician has recommended that we remove her to the seaside as soon as the roads are fit to be travelled. As such, my annual visit to your estate will commence in February, after which I shall take Georgiana to the Lake House in Ramsgate, where she might benefit from the sea air.

I do not mean to alarm you, madam. Your niece is recovering apace. I have personally seen to her care, and with the aid of my excellent housekeeper, Mrs Reynolds, we never left Georgiana unattended for a moment. I expect to see marked improvement over the next few weeks and believe she will be ready to depart as soon as the roads are passable.

Our journey from Pemberley will be a slow one, to accommodate Georgiana's condition, but I shall inform you when we reach London. Georgiana will remain in Town whilst I see to your books. She will visit the modiste for some new gowns—she has grown two inches since the summer.

After concluding my tasks at Rosings, I shall return to London to collect my sister and her companion, and we will make our way to

Ramsgate for the summer. I extend my apologies if this change in plans disrupts yours.

Until February, Aunt.

Fitzwilliam Darcy

He signed his name with more force than was necessary before sanding and sealing the letter. Darcy made no mention of his aunt's allusion to his wedding. He would not marry Anne. If he had not fallen in love with Elizabeth, duty might eventually have pushed him to offer for Anne. Thankfully, she disabused him of the notion years ago. His cousin had warned him not to ask for her hand, for she would refuse it if he did—Darcy had been relieved.

Business and estate matters consumed Darcy the remainder of the month. He worked closely with his steward to finalise plans for the spring planting, knowing he would not be present. A few tenant cottages needed repairs, and a winter storm had damaged a bridge. Through it all, Georgiana's health steadily improved, though she still had a moist cough.

Mrs Younge proved a dutiful companion, and Darcy appreciated her diligence in caring for his sister. She worked closely with Mrs Reynolds to see Georgiana well attended, and when the roads cleared enough for travel in February, there were hot bricks and plenty of rugs in the carriages to keep her charge comfortable.

Darcy delivered Georgiana and Mrs Younge to Darcy House before continuing to Rosings Park the following day. The visit was predictably intolerable, and Lady Catherine's insistence that he marry his cousin began at dinner on the very day of his arrival.

"See how lovely Anne looks, Darcy?" she remarked, lifting her soup spoon to begin her meal. "A spring wedding would be just the thing; do you not agree?"

"Spring weddings are lovely, but I will not be marrying Anne," Darcy replied evenly, not looking up from his delicious bowl of carrot soup.

Lady Catherine continued as if he had not spoken. "Mr Rawlings is getting on in years, but he can officiate your wedding. Late April would be ideal. The flowers will bloom then, and we will not need to send to London for them."

"Lady Catherine, I will *not* be marrying Anne," Darcy repeated firmly. "If you persist in this vein, I will depart in the morning and send my uncle to review your accounts."

"Why do you resist?" she blustered. "It is an ideal match on both sides. Anne is a wealthy heiress, and you are a wealthy landowner. Together, your fortunes will rival a duke's."

"I care not for wealth, madam. My cousin and I hold each other in mutual regard, but we lack the sentiments to become man and wife." He sipped his soup before continuing. "I value Anne's happiness, as well as my own, and you will not sway me."

"Anne expects your proposal!" Lady Catherine insisted.

"No, Mama, I do not," Anne said quietly from the other side of the table. "I love Darcy, but not in that way."

"Love has nothing to do with marriage! It is a business arrangement, designed to unite wealth and elevate standing. If love is what you seek, then you are a fool." Lady Catherine sniffed imperiously.

"Be that as it may, I will not marry my cousin," Darcy repeated. When his aunt made to contradict him yet again, Darcy slammed his hand on the table, causing the china to rattle, Anne to startle in her seat, and his aunt to fall silent. "Not another word," he said sharply. "If you broach this topic again, I will depart at once."

Lady Catherine's jaw clenched, but she said nothing further. The meal concluded in silence, and Darcy excused himself immediately afterwards, citing exhaustion from his journey, though he did feel bad for having behaved so aggressively during dinner

Darcy completed the account review in record time. He was determined not to remain at Rosings Park any longer than absolutely necessary, and by the eighteenth of February, he was on his way back to London to retrieve Georgiana.

His sister, with the help of Mrs Younge and Lady Matlock, had completed her shopping and was ready to depart for the Lake House as soon as Darcy gave the command. Seeing no reason to delay, they began the four-day journey on the twentieth of the month. Darcy spent much of the trip with his portable writing desk on his lap, composing a long letter to Elizabeth. He intended to place the completed missive on the salver the moment he entered the Lake House.

A cold breeze greeted them when his equipage finally trundled to a stop. He took in the green railing and chuckled at the sight of the feline tracks scattered across the threshold. The memory seemed humourous now, and he wondered if Elizabeth thought of him whenever she saw those green tracks.

"Greetings, Smythe," he said cheerfully, handing his coat and gloves to the butler. "I trust there is a fire in the parlour. We are chilled to the bone and Miss Darcy is in need of warmth."

"All is ready, sir," Smythe replied. "Cook has a tea tray waiting to be served at your request, and fires have been lit in all your chambers."

"Very good. This is Mrs Younge, Miss Darcy's companion. Have rooms been readied for her?"

"Yes, Mr Darcy. The blue room and the adjoining sitting room on the third floor has been prepared. I hope that is acceptable?"

"It is. Have Mrs Palmer show the way, will you? Georgiana, Mrs Younge, shall we have tea in a half an hour?"

The ladies agreed and followed Mrs Palmer upstairs. Darcy pulled the letter to Elizabeth from his pocket, kissed it for good measure, and dropped it onto the salver as soon as Smythe turned away. If all went well, he would have a reply from Elizabeth in a day or so. He had waited for what seemed like an eternity, and now he had only to wait a short while longer.

Chapter Sixteen

March 1, 1813
The Lake House
Ramsgate
Elizabeth

Elizabeth tickled little William's feet, and her nephew giggled madly, his legs flailing and his arms waving. Jane sat in a nearby chair, holding little Margaret and telling a silly story about a cat that could not land on its feet. It was the first of March; the weather had warmed enough to tempt Elizabeth out of doors during the afternoons. Soon it would be time for William and Margaret to rest, leaving their aunt free to seek a few hours of solitude.

Jane's health was much improved. It had taken two months before she could do more than rest and feed her babies. In early February, the children fell ill with colds, and Jane had further worn herself out nursing them through it. Elizabeth had provided constant aid, giving her sister time to rest, so she did not become ill and have to take to her bed once more.

Charles, too, took an active role in parenting his children. He was a marvellous father, crawling around the floor, reading stories, and rocking the twins to sleep. Anyone with eyes could see that he adored the babies and that his love for Jane and their family encompassed his entire being.

William began to fuss, and Elizabeth took him to the wet nurse. Jane fed Margaret, and the tiny pair were asleep within thirty minutes.

"I believe I shall go to the garden," Elizabeth told Jane. "The warm breeze beckons!"

"Be off with you," Jane chuckled. "I need to meet with Mrs Palmer to finalise our plans for the dinner party."

Elizabeth groaned. Her sister had planned an evening of entertainment for the small circle of acquaintances they had made in Ramsgate. Naturally, the guest list included the Nelsons and Mr Blandishman, along with several other couples. Elizabeth would have to spend the night paired with Mr Blandishman, since he was the only unattached gentleman invited.

"It is not so bad," Jane chided gently. "And it is only polite that we show some hospitality to our friends now that I am well again."

Elizabeth sighed and nodded. "You are right, of course. But it is not the evening that causes my pique; it is the thought of spending the entire night with Mr Blandishman by my side."

"I do not see what you find so objectionable about the gentleman." Jane regarded her sister with a concerned expression. "He may not be a wit, but he is a good man."

"Yes, he is a *'good'* man," Elizabeth replied with a touch of sarcasm—"and also egotistical, pompous, condescending, and completely uninteresting." Elizabeth crossed her arms and affected a mock pout.

"Can you find no redeeming qualities? Besides the fact that he is financially secure and an excellent match?"

Elizabeth considered. "He is thoughtful, in his own way, and seeks to please me by showing interest in my preferences... at least when he deems those preferences acceptable."

"Can you not name something without a caveat attached?"

"At the present time, *no*. I tolerate Mr Blandishman's company, but do not welcome it, I am sorry to say." She sighed inwardly. *An easy feat when one is constantly comparing him to Mr Darcy.* Once more, Elizabeth's heart longed for a word from that gentleman. It was only March—was she to survive another month without a letter? Wanting to change the subject, she added, "Really, Jane, you seem intent on seeing all others wed now that you are in that happy state! Why do you persist in thrusting me at Mr Blandishman?"

Jane laughed and waved her away. "You need not marry the man to see his *'good'* side, Lizzy. Very well, I shall cease my efforts. Go on your ramble. I am certain you will feel better when you return." Her attention returned to the ledger before her, and Elizabeth left the room without further reply.

She donned her spencer and bonnet, and as she reached for her gloves, the sight of a letter on the salver made her pause. The post had come earlier, and when there had been no letter for her, she had felt a wave of disappointment. But now—her heart quickened, as she recognised the bold, familiar script of Mr Darcy. A rush of warmth filled her chest, and she snatched the letter with trembling fingers. The forgotten gloves slipped from her hands as she hurried outside, seeking the privacy of the garden. There, hidden from view and seated on the bench under the hollowed tree, she would at last devour his words in blissful solitude.

March 1, 1811

Dear Elizabeth,

Words cannot express how relieved I will be to place this letter on the salver immediately upon my arrival at the Lake House. These months apart have been a torment, and I can scarcely write for the anticipation rising within me. There is so much to tell—so much we have left unsaid since September—and I hardly know where to begin.

Richard and I found and agreed upon a companion for Georgiana. Her name is Mrs Younge and hiring her has proven to be a boon. Georgiana is fond of her, and I have found nothing of which to complain. The lady accompanies us to Ramsgate and will continue Georgiana's education whilst we are here.

We remained in London until November, at which time we returned to Pemberley. I did something rather bold in October, and now I must ask you to search your memories from years ago as I tell you the tale.

It had not been more than a month before I missed your letters dreadfully. I contemplated travelling to Hertfordshire to contrive an introduction but recalled that you visited your relations in London when possible. More particularly, I remembered the story of your search for a book for your father's birthday. With some clever deductions, I narrowed down the time that you might have visited Hatchard's and went there daily, watching for you.

Do you remember now? I caused you to blush, so I hope I left an impression. Did you not recognise me when you first saw my likeness? I confess, I much prefer the living, breathing Elizabeth Bennet to the drawing. Your eyes are very fine—has anyone told you?

Rather than quenching my need to hear from you and be near you, that day at Hatchard's only fanned the flames of my affection. It is fortunate that necessity drove me from London, or I might have gone to Hertfordshire just to catch a glimpse of you. How strange that would have been, for time would not yet have dulled your memory of the 'besotted' gentleman at Hatchard's who so kindly assisted you in securing a book for your father.

Winters in Derbyshire can be long. I kept myself occupied with letters of business and tenant matters whilst impatiently waiting for the time to pass. Then, after Christmas, Georgiana fell ill. Her condition was bleak for some nights, but at last the fever broke. She retained a lingering cough, and so I resolved then to take her to Ramsgate as soon as the weather warmed enough for her to travel. I moved my annual journey to Rosings Park from April to February, and, as I write these words, now we are trundling down the road towards the Lake House.

The visit with Lady Catherine was predictably tense. I disabused her of the notion that Anne and I will ever marry. I wonder if this visit to Ramsgate is the reason she claims, in your present day, that Anne will never marry. My aunt and I did not part amicably, though she did allow me to kiss her farewell. Time will tell, I suppose.

Did your sister come through her confinement in good health? How is your new niece or nephew?

I close this letter now and look forward to hearing from you as soon as may be. Pray, do not keep me waiting long, for I fear I cannot bear it.

Yours,

Fitzwilliam Darcy

Elizabeth let out an unladylike squeal and hugged the letter to her chest. He had missed her—at least as much as she had missed him! And now he was here, a full month before he had hoped to be. And to think that she had already met him! Elizabeth struggled to recall the man's features from their meeting at Hatchard's, as the memories had faded. She remembered her unaccountable shyness as he regarded her, making it impossible for her to look into his face for long. That had been Mr Darcy! He had known who she was and arranged to meet her. It was very romantic. She now understood why his likeness had seemed vaguely familiar to her.

But how dreadful for Miss Darcy to have been so ill! She hoped the young lady would wholly recover soon. Elizabeth knew how devastating it was to watch a loved one suffer.

She did not linger in the garden. Instead, she returned to the house and went to her chamber, determined to waste no time replying to Mr Darcy.

March 1, 1813

Dear Mr Darcy,
Your letter could not have arrived at a more opportune time. My dear sister wonders why I resist the attentions of an honourable man. She has rightly observed that I have not attempted to appreciate Mr Blandishman's merits, but I find it difficult to do so when comparing him to another gentleman of my acquaintance.

I am so pleased that you have returned and hasten to respond to your missive. Jane came through her confinement alive—a bold statement, perhaps, but there was a brief time when the midwife was deeply concerned. However, I am pleased to say that we Bennets are of hearty stock, and my sister has now recovered from her difficult pregnancy and delivery. She is hardly any worse for wear, though the midwife wonders if Jane will carry another child.

As for the babe, there were two! Yes, I am the proud aunt of a niece and a nephew. William Charles was born first, followed by Margaret Elizabeth. William has tawny locks with hints of red, and his sister had dark hair that has lightened considerably in the last months. Both are amiable, just like their parents, and I take much delight in spending my hours entertaining them.

We spent our winter at the Lake House. We did not attend parties or soirees, for Jane's recovery has been abominably slow. By January, she was still abed for much of the day, though she has now regained most of her strength. The children, thankfully, were in health, save for a brief cold. The poor dears were miserable until it passed.

Charles and Jane will host a dinner party in two weeks and are inviting all the new acquaintances we have made in Ramsgate. It will be the first time they have formally entertained at the Lake House. Jane's condition and recovery after the births prohibited us from having guests. I did not mind the solitude. I fear I am becoming like my father, for the thought of having a house full of guests holds little appeal for me. I would rather hide in my room with a book.

I will deposit this on the salver immediately, hoping you will have it soon. Are we still to meet in April, or shall we move the date forward?

Yours sincerely,

E. Bennet

Elizabeth sanded and sealed the letter. Her heart was lighter than it had been in a long while. The prospect of finally meeting the man she had been writing to for months filled her with anticipation. She carried the letter downstairs and placed it on the salver before returning to the garden for quiet reflection.

The lavender had just begun to show new green shoots, but it would be many months before the plant bloomed again. Yet even in its dormant state, it reminded her of Mr Darcy's approbation, and she took comfort in that.

Her thoughts turned to the last letter he had written before leaving Ramsgate the previous autumn: *Your wit and vivacity have enchanted me; I am under your spell... I love you. Wait for me.*

Elizabeth smiled softly to herself. She loved him too, though she had yet to say the words. She could not deny it. The mere thought of living without him brought pain to her chest and agony to her soul. She would tell him, and soon, but not in a letter. It seemed only right to wait and share her heart in person, to see the delight and love in his eyes as she spoke her deepest feelings to him—and to hear him say her name as he returned her sentiments.

Their correspondence resumed with enthusiasm, and the back and forth of letters across the two years that separated them began anew. Mr Darcy quickly agreed to move their meeting forward, and they settled upon the sixteenth of March, the day after Jane's dinner party. Mr Darcy, ever considerate, assured Elizabeth he did not wish to intrude upon the Lake House before then, having no desire to impose upon her brother and sister. The date suited Elizabeth perfectly; it gave her something to think on as she endured Mr Blandishman's company throughout the evening. The day after the dinner, she would take James or John with her to Mrs Peacock's tearoom and finally meet Mr Darcy.

The fifteenth of March dawned beautifully. The staff at the Lake House bustled about, making final preparations, and ensuring all was ready. Jane reviewed the last of the details whilst Elizabeth tended to her niece and nephew. Her sister had insisted that she needed no other aid. The wet nurse and maid would manage the twins during the evening, but Jane was loath to leave their care in others' hands more than necessary.

An hour before the guests would arrive, Susan helped Elizabeth dress. She donned a gown of sage green sarsenet and a string of lustrous pearls. Her maid arranged her hair fashionably, dotting the locks with matching pearl hairpins. Elbow-length gloves completed the ensemble, and Elizabeth made her way to the parlour where Jane would receive their guests.

Her sister was waiting. Jane looked exquisitely lovely, her modish attire enhancing her natural beauty. It was clear to anyone who saw her why Charles had fallen so deeply in love. Those who truly knew her, however, understood that her inner beauty was just as captivating as her outward appearance.

"There you are!" Jane smiled as Elizabeth entered the room. Charles arrived shortly after and approached his wife, kissing her cheek tenderly.

"You look ravishing, my dear," he said. "I shall be the envy of every man here tonight. Is all ready?"

Jane nodded, smiling serenely. "I will have dinner served at seven. Whilst we dine, the servants will set up the card tables. After that, tea and coffee will conclude the evening."

"It sounds as though you have everything well managed." Charles squeezed Jane's hand, and Elizabeth's heart tightened. *Tomorrow*, she reminded herself. *Tomorrow it is your turn.*

The bell rang, and Jane smoothed the front of her gown. She moved to the door with Charles, ready to welcome their first guest. Elizabeth glanced at the clock on the mantel. They did not expect any guests for another half hour. Who had come so early?

Smythe entered the room with Mr Blandishman at his side, and it took all of Elizabeth's restraint not to groan aloud. *Of course,* she griped inwardly. *Who else would lack the social graces to arrive so far before the appointed hour?*

Mr Blandishman moved to Elizabeth's side immediately after greeting Mr and Mrs Bingley. "How do you do this evening, Miss Bennet?" he asked, scooping up her hand and bowing over it. "It has been a week since we were last in company. Have you been keeping busy?"

"I spend my time with my niece and nephew." Elizabeth repeated her practised answer, knowing full well he would commend her for her dedication before enquiring when they might walk again.

She was not wrong. He did just that, and she evaded the question by claiming a need to excuse herself for a moment. Elizabeth left the room and found refuge in a small alcove by the stairs, seeking to regain her equanimity. Her irritation with the gentleman was not entirely sound; he had done nothing that evening to deserve her ire. Yet, she found his predictability tiresome, and his bland personality more of a trial that evening than it ever had been before.

This most certainly stems from the fact that I am to meet Mr Darcy tomorrow, she reasoned with herself. *I can tolerate a bore for one more evening. It is no remarkable feat.* Taking a deep breath, Elizabeth steeled herself for the remainder of the night. With a smile fixed firmly in place, she rejoined the occupants of the parlour. Two more couples had joined the gathering, and she greeted them warmly before moving in the opposite direction of Mr Blandishman. Her subtle attempts proved futile, however, as the gentleman soon made his way back to her side.

"Have I told you about the letter I received from my cousin, Miss Bennet?" he began. "He is in Ireland and has let a lovely cottage for the summer..." Mr Blandishman continued speaking, leaving Elizabeth little opportunity to reply beyond a nod or the occasional noncommittal murmur.

Mr Blandishman kept her constant company through dinner, cards, and tea. By the end of the evening, Elizabeth felt utterly drained from the effort of maintaining civility and retreated directly to her bed, embracing the sweet oblivion that sleep promised.

Elizabeth awoke the next morning filled with anticipation. It was nine o'clock, much later than she normally rose, but she had no regret. There were only three hours until she would be at the tea shop with Mr Darcy. She hurried through her ablutions and through breakfast, only to find herself at sixes and sevens as time crawled slowly towards noon.

At last, at half-past eleven, she informed Jane of her plans and prepared to depart.

"Bring me some pastries, will you, Lizzy?" Charles asked from behind his newspaper. Elizabeth agreed and hurried from the room.

She asked John to accompany her and set a brisk pace as they strolled down streets towards Mrs Peacock's shop. She arrived with five minutes to spare and looked for a seat. Mr Darcy had mentioned a particular spot by the window that offered a splendid view of the ocean, and Elizabeth chose a table there. John lingered outside on a bench, near enough to see her but far enough to give her a measure of privacy.

"Good afternoon, madam," a shop assistant said. "What may I bring you?"

Elizabeth quickly ordered the pastries for Charles and a few things for herself. Mr Darcy would no doubt wish to procure his own preferences. She nibbled at her selection as the clock in the shop chimed first noon, then a quarter past twelve, and then half past twelve. With each passing quarter hour, her anxiety grew, and she found herself glancing at the door more frequently. When the clock struck one, doubts began to creep into her thoughts. By two, Elizabeth had finished both her order and Charles's. A serving girl had refilled her tea several times, and she had ordered refreshments for John also.

As Elizabeth sat by the window, waiting, she noticed Mrs. Peacock bustling around the tea shop, her joy evident in every smile she gave her patrons. Earlier, the proprietor had ensured Elizabeth was comfortable, offering a cheerful recommendation for the day's pastries. Mrs Peacock made sure every patron was satisfied, offering a kind word here, a plate of fresh pastries there, her laughter occasionally ringing through the air like music. It was no wonder Mr Darcy had spoken of her with such fondness. She exuded joy, just like he had said.

By the time the clock neared three, Mrs Peacock approached her table once more, her brow furrowed with concern. "You have been here a long while, my dear," she said kindly. "Is everything all right?" Elizabeth forced a smile, though her heart was heavy. "I was expecting someone, but it appears they will not come."

Mrs. Peacock's eyes softened. "I see. Do let me know if you need anything else."

Elizabeth nodded, and with a sympathetic smile, Mrs. Peacock moved on, leaving Elizabeth to gather her thoughts in the quiet of her disappointment.

At three, she had no choice but to accept the truth: Mr Darcy was not coming. She rose dejectedly, weighed down with the deepest disillusionment, and made her way outside. As if to match her mood, the heavens opened, and she and John were thoroughly drenched by the time they reached the Lake House.

"There you are, Lizzy!" Jane cried as they entered. "We had quite despaired of you! Come, let us get you dry! You are soaked through. You too, John, go and change."

Elizabeth shivered as Jane ushered her upstairs to her chamber, where Susan was waiting with a fresh gown. The maid swiftly removed her sodden clothes and wrapped a shawl around her shoulders.

"I will ring for some tea," Jane said as she guided Elizabeth to a chair near the fire. "A footman has stoked the flames to warm you whilst you wait." Her sister bustled away, no doubt to call for a tray.

Elizabeth said nothing. She stared into the fire, her mind racing over every conversation, every hope, and every dream of the past months. He had not come. She had waited, but he had not come. Surely, something vital must have kept him away—he had promised so faithfully.

She sank into the plush cushions as her first tears fell. Not wishing to speak with anyone, she stood, walked to her bed, and slipped beneath the coverlet, pulling it tightly around her. She rolled onto her side, facing away from the door. When Jane entered with Sally, Elizabeth feigned sleep until her sister and the maid left. Only when the room fell silent did she allow herself to truly weep.

Elizabeth longed to write to Mr Darcy, to demand why he had not come, but it was a futile thought. The Mr Darcy of 1811 would know no more than she why his future self had failed her. Was he ill? Was he married? Was he waylaid by highwaymen? It was impossible to know.

As she lay on her pillows, her tears subsided, and calm resignation settled over her. She had suspended her very existence for him. It was time to let go.

Chapter Seventeen

March 18, 1811
The Lake House
Ramsgate
Darcy

Darcy waited impatiently for the post, eager for a letter from Elizabeth. Had they met in 1813? How had it gone? Would she stop writing now that their acquaintance had reached her present? Questions plagued his mind, but above all, he hoped to hear that all was well, and his future self had proposed to her.

The post arrived just before luncheon, and Darcy quickly sifted through the letters until he found one from Elizabeth. Hastily breaking the seal, he began to read.

March 17, 1813

My dear Mr Darcy,
I find I do not entirely know how to write this letter. I imagine this is how you felt when you first realised our communication spanned time, though I write, perhaps, with more despondency than you did then.

You did not come. I waited at Mrs Peacock's shop for three hours, but you never arrived. It is impossible to know what kept you from our appointment, for you are in the past and have no notion of your future self's actions. There are many possible explanations for your absence, but the most likely is that you are married and can no longer keep your promise to me. It fits, does it not? Did Lady Catherine not allude to such during my visit to Rosings Park in the spring of 1812? You are a gentleman of worth, capable of securing any lady's affections when you put forth the effort.

It is best that we cease our communication entirely, for to continue would only prolong the agony I now feel. I release you from any obligation you might have felt, as you have so eloquently expressed your sentiments in past missives. We must both move on and seek our happiness in our own time.

Before I close, I must take this opportunity to speak from my heart, for I may never get another chance. Almost from the first letter, you fascinated me. Piece by piece, word by word, I lost my heart to you until it was irrevocably gone. How cruel of fate to grant me the exquisite felicity of loving you only to snatch it away before we could begin a life together? I love you, Mr Fitzwilliam Darcy of Pemberley, not for your name or your social status, but for your kindness, your compassion, your attentiveness, and your dedication. I love you for your commitment to your sister, for your sense of honour and duty. I love you for allowing a silly country girl into your life and treating her as your equal and as an intelligent human being. I love you, and I will never feel such depths of emotion for another.

Be happy, Mr Darcy, for me, and for yourself. Find joy in your life and in fulfilling your responsibilities. And when you meet the lady who eclipses me in your heart, embrace her fully and do not delay.

I, too, must find another. Until now, I have stubbornly resisted the attentions of a certain man. Perhaps I was too dismissive of him because I filled my heart with you. Though I have no intention of encouraging Mr Blandishman, I now see that if I were to be courted by anyone, I must first let go of the past. No doubt I will find someone suitable if I allow myself the opportunity.

Since writing the above, I have learned that Jane and Charles's lease ends in July and will not be renewed. My brother mentioned that the family wishes to use the Lake House this summer, and so we must depart. As I am at their disposal, I imagine I will accompany them back to Netherfield Park. It has been nearly a year since I have seen my family, and I welcome the reunion.

Do not despair, Mr Darcy. I will be well. When you bring your family to the Lake House, share with them all that you once shared with me. Retrieve the snuff box, tell its story, and return Miss Darcy's music to her. Above all, remember me as you sit amongst the lavender.

Adieu,

Elizabeth Bennet

Darcy raked a hand through his hair, panic rising within him. He had not come. But how? What had kept him from her? Elizabeth's letter sounded so final, but surely, she could not mean what she said. Could she? Was this truly the end?

He hurriedly grabbed a fresh sheet of paper and penned a reply, his hand shaking as he sealed it sloppily. In his letter, he begged her to reconsider, to not give up so easily. *Any number of incidents could have kept me away*, he wrote. *Perhaps I forgot we had changed the date and did not plan to arrive until April.*

But no answer came.

A week passed, and Darcy wrote again, his desperation growing. Still, nothing. By the first week of April, he sent yet another letter, his hope slipping away with each passing day. Time stretched on, each hour feeling like a lifetime. The silence from Elizabeth was unbearable.

Darcy poured over her letters, each word becoming an obsession. Her last letter haunted him the most. She hinted at giving another man a chance to win her heart. No, it could not be! He had to stop her.

A letter arrived from his friend Charles Bingley in mid-April, containing an invitation to join him at his brother-in-law's estate in Surrey. Darcy was in the midst of composing a reply to decline when Georgiana approached him.

"Who do you write to, Brother?" she asked, her voice tinged with a tentative curiosity, as though she feared provoking a sharp response.

"Bingley," he replied, glancing at her. "He invites me to Surrey for a few months. I am declining."

"Why ever for?" Georgiana's brow furrowed in confusion. "You are not happy here; that much is clear. You have been distracted and distant since mid-March. I can scarcely persuade you to speak, let alone smile or laugh."

"When did you become so observant?" he teased, though with little conviction.

"Go, Brother," Georgiana urged gently. "Mrs Younge is here with me, and I am perfectly content to stay here at the Lake House. If it will lift your spirits, I am all in favour."

Darcy frowned, weighing Georgiana's words. Consumed by the misery of Elizabeth's silence, he failed to realise how his melancholy had affected his sister. "Very well," he said at last. "But I shall return in time for your birthday."

Georgiana leaned forward and kissed his cheek. "I hope Surrey brings you some resolution to your troubles," she said softly. "I love you."

"I love you, too, Poppet," he replied, managing a small smile.

A letter to Bingley was promptly sent, arranging a place where they could meet and travel the remainder of their journey together. Three days later, Darcy bid his sister farewell, reminding her to write weekly, and boarded his carriage.

He met Bingley in London, and his friend's cheerful disposition instantly began to lift the weight of Darcy's depressed spirits.

"How do you do, Darcy?" Bingley greeted him as they met at the coaching inn. "It has been an age, has it not? My sisters are eager to see you again."

Darcy groaned inwardly. He ought to have realised that Miss Bingley would be in attendance, which meant he would have to dodge her clawing advances for the next two months. "It certainly has been an eventful year. I can scarcely believe how quickly time has passed since we were last in each other's company. Your elder sister has married—has the younger formed an attachment yet?"

"Yes, the Hursts wed in Scarborough around Christmas. She seems content with her lot, which is all a brother could hope for. Caroline has no prospects as of yet, but I am hopeful for the new season. How fares your dear sister?"

"She is well now, though she was quite ill this winter. Georgiana remains in Ramsgate with her companion." Darcy shifted in his seat, feeling a nagging unease that had lingered since Bingley first wrote in April. What was it?

"Capital! I am pleased to hear it. You know, I have finally decided upon leasing an estate. I am not yet ready to purchase, and I believe leasing will provide me with valuable experience without the commitment." Bingley grinned, clearly proud of his decision.

"That is a fine idea," Darcy agreed. "Have you sent out inquiries?"

His friend shrugged. "A few. I was rather hoping to prevail upon you to help me view and select an estate when the time comes."

"Of course." Darcy nodded, and Bingley resumed his cheerful chatter. As in the past, Darcy was grateful for his friend's loquacious nature, which allowed him time to reflect. Unfortunately, his thoughts too often turned to a certain lady from Hertfordshire with exceptionally fine eyes and a rapier-sharp wit. Despite her assertion that he would meet someone else and marry, he knew deep within his heart that he could neither forget her nor forsake her. He briefly considered traveling to Meryton to woo her and win her hand, but Richard's concerns over what would happen resounded in his memory, preventing him from acting on that impulse.

Even so, Darcy resolved to honour Elizabeth's wishes that they move on with their lives. He would begin during his time in Surrey.

Darcy's visit to the Hurst estate tested both his patience and self-control. More than once, he found himself tempted to rebuke Miss Bingley for her possessive and shrew-like behaviour. Instead, he sought refuge in secluded corners of the house, doing all he could to avoid being alone with her.

Inevitably, his thoughts would turn to Elizabeth. Both women were handsome, but Miss Bingley's beauty lacked the warmth and vivacity that Elizabeth's presence carried. Where Miss Bingley's words were often sharp and cruel, Elizabeth had always sought to be polite and gracious, even when she found someone's company disagreeable.

Miss Bingley, however, was relentless. She frequently urged her brother to hasten his search for an estate, so convinced that his elevation to landowner would increase her chances of becoming *Mrs Darcy*. Bingley always responded with his usual cheer, reminding his sister that he was still waiting for further enquiries.

One morning, as Bingley sifted through his post, he exclaimed with enthusiasm. "See here, Darcy! I believe I have found a promising prospect. My solicitor writes of a house just three hours north of London, available come September. It has been undergoing repairs for the past year and stands empty during the renovations."

"A prospect so close to London is certainly worth investigating," Darcy remarked. "Do you not have business concerns in Town?"

Miss Bingley laughed. "Business concerns? No, my brother would never!"

"Do not be ridiculous, Caroline," Bingley replied. "Even Darcy has business in London."

Darcy nodded, noting Miss Bingley's flushed cheeks. Whether it was from irritation or mortification, he could not say.

"What is the name of the place?" Hurst asked lazily from his reclining position on the sofa.

"Netherfield Park."

It was as if a bolt of lightning had struck Darcy. A complete shock gripped him, and in an instant, what had been gnawing at him since Elizabeth's last letter fell into place.

"Pray, excuse me for a moment," Darcy said abruptly. "I just recalled a matter that requires my attention. When I return, you can tell me more of Netherfield Park."

With that, Darcy hurried from the room, making his way swiftly to his chambers. There, he unearthed Elizabeth's letters from the bottom of his trunk. He began at the first and hastily scanned each one. Not once had she mentioned her sister's married name—not even in her very last.

Darcy read the line again: *I have learned, since writing the above, Jane and Charles's lease is up at the end of July and not to be renewed.* There it was, clear in Elizabeth's elegant hand—and scattered throughout her previous letters the name *Netherfield Park* appeared. This was it. Somehow, in his desperation, he had glossed over it. What were the odds that Bingley had leased Netherfield Park in Hertfordshire, married her sister Jane, and unwittingly brought Darcy closer to Elizabeth once more?

A spark of hope flared within him. Could Fate truly be offering him another chance to be with Elizabeth?

Darcy pondered what to do. He had intended to return to Georgiana the next week, but an urgent desire to leave sooner swelled within him. Elizabeth was to quit Ramsgate at the end of July. If he departed tomorrow, he could send a letter to her before she left, explaining what he had just discovered. Perhaps it would give her enough hope—enough to prevent her from considering Mr Blandishman, or any other suitor.

He gathered the letters and returned them to the trunk, calling for his valet to pack for an early departure. Georgiana would not be expecting him, but he was certain she would welcome the surprise.

With his decision made, Darcy rejoined Bingley in the parlour. "I regret to say I must leave tomorrow," he told his friend apologetically. Cries of protest came from Miss Bingley and the Hursts. Darcy ignored them, continuing to speak to Bingley. "But tell me—what more can you share of Netherfield Park? It sounds promising."

Bingley launched into a detailed account of the estate, listing its attractions and potential. Darcy listened attentively, offering encouragement. "It seems a fitting prospect for you," he agreed. "I shall return to London in August. If you wish, I could ride and assess the property with you."

Bingley's eyes lit up. "Better still, Darcy, you must promise to be my guest for some months! Your expertise and company would be invaluable."

Darcy smiled, nodding. "Done. You may count on my presence."

Miss Bingley looked far too pleased by this agreement, which prompted Darcy to rise. "Now, if you will excuse me, I must attend to my packing. It is a long journey back to Ramsgate, and I wish to surprise my dear sister before her birthday."

Bidding his farewells, Darcy left the room. The sun was barely rising the next morning when his carriage set off from Hurst's estate. It would be just a matter of time now. If Elizabeth did not reply to his letter upon his return to Ramsgate, he would see her in September.

Chapter Eighteen

July 15, 1813
The Lake House
Ramsgate
Elizabeth

Elizabeth strolled through the park, her hand resting lightly on Mr Blandishman's arm as he rambled on. She nodded absently whenever he seemed to need a response, her thoughts elsewhere. The objections she had voiced over the past months had faded—or perhaps she had simply grown more tolerant of his company. There was nothing *overtly wrong* with the gentleman; he was neither evil nor wholly undesirable. And whilst she did not love him, she had developed an awkward sort of affection for him. Mr Blandishman, for his part, had seemingly accepted that Elizabeth's feelings would never deepen beyond friendship. He no longer pressed for more and now only called at the Lake House once or twice a week.

Elizabeth was relieved that particular burden had lifted. She knew it would be many years before another could truly touch her affections. Mr Darcy still filled her thoughts and heart, and no one could claim the space he held within her.

Her sister and brother appeared unaware of Elizabeth's subtle change in demeanour. The once cheerful and optimistic young woman had become a quieter, more sedate version of herself. Her spirits, though not outwardly troubled, had become undeniably dimmed. She believed she masked her sorrow well, but from time to time, she noticed a flicker of concern in Smythe's gaze. The faithful butler continued to deliver the post to her personally, even though Mrs Bingley had long since assumed full management of the household. Perhaps he hoped that a letter from a friend would bring Elizabeth comfort. But Elizabeth carefully hid the letters Mr Darcy continued to send, even from Smythe. And not even Jane knew of the secret correspondence that still bound Elizabeth to the man she loved but could never have.

The Bingleys walked ahead, leaving enough distance to afford some measure of privacy whilst still maintaining proper chaperonage. Elizabeth's thoughts drifted, her mind wandering to the unopened letters hidden at the bottom of her trunk.

Mr Darcy had not ceased writing to her, despite her farewell. His once-steady handwriting had grown increasingly erratic, at least on the exterior of the missives. Elizabeth could not to bring herself to open any of his letters, the wound in her heart still too raw. She longed to heal, but to do so, she knew she could not continue to open the wound by revisiting his words. Eventually, the letters had ceased, but rather than bring her relief, it had only compounded her distress.

"Ho there!" Bingley cried out, brimming with delight. Elizabeth immediately snapped back to the present, her gaze following her brother's enthusiastic wave towards a fashionably dressed couple yet approaching from the distance.

"Colonel Fitzwilliam! Miss Darcy! How do you do? I never thought to see you here!" Bingley bowed, then eagerly shook the gentleman's hand.

Hearing their names drew Elizabeth's attention. Miss Darcy was everything her brother had described—tall, graceful, and poised. The man beside her, Colonel Fitzwilliam, was clearly Mr Darcy's cousin, the very man of whom he had written so often.

"How do you do, Bingley?" the colonel replied, his smile broad and easy. "It has been far too long, has it not?"

"More than a year," Bingley agreed, his cheerful expression sobering as he stepped aside. "May I introduce my wife, Mrs Jane Bingley, her sister Miss Elizabeth Bennet, and Mr John Blandishman."

A glint flickered in Colonel Fitzwilliam's eyes, and for a moment, Elizabeth wondered if Mr Darcy had confided in him. But the notion was discarded quickly—who would believe such an extraordinary tale?

"What brings you to Ramsgate?" Charles asked. "Will you join us at our home?"

"We have come for the summer," Miss Darcy answered. "My cousin and I are staying at the hotel until the tenants vacate the Lake House. Afterwards, we will make preparations for its sale."

Jane gasped, her eyes wide with surprise, but Elizabeth remained composed. She had known all along who owned the home they had been leasing.

"Why, we are leasing Lake House!" Bingley exclaimed, visibly shaken. "I had no idea. My solicitor handled all the paperwork, and I did not know the identity of the owners."

Mr Blandishman interrupted the conversation with a regretful look. "I fear I must take my leave. I have an engagement that cannot be delayed." He bowed politely to the group, bidding them a good day before striding briskly away.

"We would be pleased to take tea with you," the colonel said, "but unfortunately, we have a prior engagement as well. Tomorrow, perhaps?"

"That would be most agreeable," Jane answered, her tone warm and welcoming. "Shall we expect you at two o'clock?"

With the arrangements made, Miss Darcy and Colonel Fitzwilliam took their leave, and Elizabeth found herself trailing behind her brother and sister on the walk back to the Lake House. They had scarcely stepped inside when Charles's agitation became evident.

"Had I known who owned Lake House, I could not have dwelt here with any equanimity," he burst out, looking truly distressed. Jane immediately slipped her arm through his, guiding him to the sofa.

"What is it, Charles?" she asked softly, her voice full of concern. Elizabeth seated herself in a nearby chair, her attention fixed entirely on her brother-in-law.

Charles drew a deep breath. "Do you recall when we first met? I was… not quite myself. I had recently suffered a terrible loss."

"Yes, you could not speak of it," Jane said gently. "Will you tell us now?"

Charles nodded; his expression was sombre. "I was friends with Miss Darcy's brother. Fitzwilliam Darcy was as good a man as you could find—and an even better friend. He was a dedicated brother, a fair master, a responsible landlord, and a shrewd businessman. Despite my humble origins, we formed a strong bond of friendship. In fact, it was he who encouraged me to lease Netherfield Park." Charles reached for Jane's hand, his eyes reflecting his love for her. "It is he for whom our son—William—is named."

"He was staying with me that summer at my brother's estate in Surrey. Darcy was... not himself. His moods were dark, and I could see the constant strain that marred his countenance. I thought it was because he had left Miss Darcy in Ramsgate, but I had the sense that there was more to it."

Guilt stabbed at Elizabeth's heart. *She* was the reason Darcy had been morose that summer.

Charles lifted his gaze to the ceiling, as if searching his memory, before continuing. "After hearing of Netherfield, his spirits seemed to rally, and he even resolved to visit once I had settled the estate. But the next day, he left for Ramsgate to see his sister... and I never saw him again."

His voice faltered as he wiped at his eyes. "I do not know all the particulars. From what I have heard, when he arrived, Darcy found a man in the house. The whole of the ton was buzzing with the story for months. It was said the man was a paramour to Miss Darcy's companion. Darcy confronted him, and they fought. During the scuffle, Darcy was pushed—he fell and struck his head... and never regained consciousness."

Charles paused, the weight of his sorrow evident. "They hanged the dastard not long after, though I do not recall the official charge."

Elizabeth struggled to breathe. Her vision blurred with spots as she fought to maintain her equilibrium. "I shall call for tea," she managed, standing abruptly. Her departure went unnoticed, Jane still occupied with comforting her distraught husband.

Her mind whirling, Elizabeth rushed to the parlour where her writing case lay. She did not bother to be neat; urgency fuelled her as she hastily scrawled a note to Mr Darcy. It was the fifteenth of July. If there was any justice in the world—any higher power watching over them—she prayed that this letter would reach Mr Darcy's waiting hands in time.

July 15, 1811
The Lake House
Ramsgate
Darcy

Darcy entered the house and removed his hat and gloves. The silence unnerved him, and he wondered where Smythe and the footmen had gone. As he placed his gloves inside his hat, his eyes caught sight of the salver—and froze. There, resting on the otherwise empty tray, was a letter. The handwriting was instantly familiar. Without hesitation, he snatched it up, all thoughts of greeting Georgiana forgotten.

July 15, 1813

My dear Mr Darcy,
I pray this letter reaches you in time. Today has been otherworldly, and I finally understand why you did not come in March. You did not come because you could *not. Allow me to explain.*
Today, whilst strolling in the park with my sister and her husband, we encountered your sister and your cousin, Colonel Fitzwilliam. The meeting was stilted and somewhat awkward, and left Charles overcome

with emotion when we returned to the Lake House. I did not know you and my brother were friends, or I would have mentioned it sooner! He did not realise this house was yours and has now told Jane and me everything.

When you return to Ramsgate in 1811, you will find an intruder in your home. Charles says the man has some improper connexion to Miss Darcy's companion, though much of the incident has been deliberately hushed. There will be an altercation—during which... you lose your life! You die, Fitzwilliam! I cannot even begin to describe how it feels to write those words, to imagine a world where you no longer exist.

That is why you did not come! You are neither married nor ill. I beg you, if this letter finds you before that fateful moment, seek aid and do not confront the intruder. You must stop him. Find help. Do not face him alone—please! Once you have expelled the blackguard and secured your house, know that I am here waiting. Pray, wait for me. I am here at the Lake House, waiting for you.

Love,

Elizabeth

Darcy reread the missive, his eyes lingering on Elizabeth's words before he slowly lifted his gaze towards the empty hallway. Moving silently through the house, he searched for Smythe or Mrs Palmer, but found neither. His steps finally took him to the kitchens, where he discovered James and John sharing a meal with Cook.

"Master!" James cried, rising quickly to his feet.

"James," Darcy acknowledged. "Where is everyone?"

"Mrs Younge gave us a free afternoon," John supplied. "She does that every Wednesday. Tells us to go out, she does. 'Enjoy the day and see yer families,' she says."

"And yet you and your brother remain."

James shrugged. "We stayed in, sir."

Darcy's frown deepened, his thoughts whirling. He glanced down at the crumpled paper still clutched in his hand, and with a quick motion, gestured to the burly footmen. "Come with me," he ordered. The twins exchanged uneasy glances but obeyed as Darcy led the way back to the public rooms. Voices filtered through the corridor, and as he recognised the intruder's voice, his blood ran cold.

He threw open the door, fury rising as he took in the sight before him. George Wickham sat in his parlour, with Georgiana perched on his lap. Wickham had his arms around Darcy's sister, with his chin resting insolently on her shoulder.

His vision clouded with rage, the letter in Darcy's hand crumpling further into his tightening fist. *I am here at the Lake House, waiting for you.* Elizabeth's plea echoed in his mind. He stepped forward but paused as Wickham and Georgiana turned to face him.

"Brother!" Georgiana exclaimed, pulling out of the blackguard's embrace and standing. She came towards her brother. "You have come! Now I need not marry without you!"

"James, John," Darcy said coldly, his voice steady despite the fury bubbling beneath. "Detain Mr Wickham."

The twins stepped forward and seized his foe by the arms, pulling him out of his seat. Wickham struggled briefly but stilled when it became clear he would not easily escape them.

"No!" Georgiana protested. "We are betrothed, Fitzwilliam! You must be kind. George has explained everything to me—your past quarrels—and he wishes to make amends. Set aside your resentful temper for one moment and allow him to speak!"

Darcy's lips curled into a bitter smile. "Will you tell her, or shall I, George?" he asked, sarcasm lacing each word.

Georgiana looked between the two men, her eyes wide with uncertainty. "B-brother?" she stammered. "George said you would object.

We were to go to Gretna Green in two days. Was he right? Will you now deny your blessing, knowing that we love each other?"

"Did Wickham tell you why I would object to your marrying him? Did he tell you he has squandered a legacy of four thousand pounds? Or that he has left women ruined—from ladies to servants—across Lambton and London alike? Did he tell you he came here last year to claim the living he abandoned, vowing revenge when I refused? Did he tell you he is penniless? And do *you* realise that if you marry him without the protection of a marriage settlement, he will have complete access to your dowry, leaving you utterly at his mercy?"

Georgiana paled as Darcy spoke the hard truths his sister needed to hear. "Where is your companion?" he asked quietly.

"She has gone out," Georgiana whispered, barely audible. "She always does. Mrs Younge says it is perfectly acceptable since we are... *were* betrothed."

"I will deal with her when she returns. Go to your room, Georgie. I need to remove this miscreant from our home."

Georgiana burst into tears and fled the room. James and John stepped forward, hauling Wickham to his feet. "I ought to flay you alive," Darcy hissed, low and menacing. "I ought to see you rot in Marshalsea for every debt I have paid on your behalf."

"But you will not," Wickham sneered. "Your memories of your father hold you too much in thrall." Wickham yanked his arm free, his elbow slamming into John's face and opening a deep cut above his eye. The footman, startled by the blow, loosened his grip. Wickham struggled wildly in James's hold, raining punches on the other man with his free hand. As James tried to hold on, Wickham managed one final wrench, freeing himself from the grasp but losing his balance in the process. He stumbled towards the fireplace, tripped over the edge of the hearth, and crashed headfirst into the gilded corner of the mantle. Darcy cringed inwardly as the sound of bone meeting wood echoed through the room. He watched in horror as Wickham crumpled to the floor, blood pouring from the gash in his forehead.

Darcy knelt beside his childhood friend, checking for any sign of life. Wickham's chest lay still, his breath no longer rising or falling. Sighing, he stood and turned to John, who sat holding a bloodied handkerchief to his injured eye.

Darcy handed his loyal servant a fresh cloth from his own pocket. John grimaced in thanks and replaced the soiled one. "I am sorry I did not step in to assist you," he said.

"No matter, sir. You'll have no trouble tellin' the two of us apart now, sir," John joked half-heartedly.

"What shall we do with him, Mr Darcy?" James asked, jerking his head towards the body on the floor.

"Summon the undertaker," he replied wearily. "I shall handle all the arrangements." James nodded and disappeared out the door.

Darcy barely had a moment to breathe when the door swung open, and Mrs. Younge appeared. Her eyes widened as she took in the scene—Wickham's body, John's bloodied face, and Darcy's cold stare.

"Mr. Darcy, what—what has happened?" she stammered.

Darcy straightened. "You know full well what has happened, Mrs. Younge," he said icily. "You allowed this. You abandoned your duty, left my sister vulnerable, and now we see the result."

"I—I didn't know—"

"You knew enough," Darcy interrupted, his voice sharp. "You will leave this house at once. Be assured, Mrs. Younge, you will not find respectable employment again."

Her face paled, and without another word, she turned and fled.

As John went to fetch ice from the icehouse, Darcy retreated to his chambers to gather his wits. His thoughts were in turmoil. He still clutched Elizabeth's letter, realising the profound impact they had each just made on their future. What would happen next, he could not say, but come September, he *would* see her.

Chapter Nineteen

July 15, 1813
The Lake House
Ramsgate
Elizabeth

Elizabeth paced the music room in agitation. It had been an hour since she left the letter on the salver. Upon checking, she discovered the letter had vanished, and she prayed Darcy had found it in 1811 before the disaster struck. Her restlessness grew and grew until she could bear it no longer. Instead of pacing, she moved to the pianoforte and played the music she had long ago retrieved from its hiding place.

The notes soothed her soul; she had mastered the piece a while ago after nearly six months of constant practise, and each time she heard the familiar strains, her unusual courtship with Mr Darcy replayed in her mind.

As the final chords of the song trailed off, an unfamiliar yet familiar voice spoke from the doorway.

"I swore when I hid that music years ago that I would tear it to shreds if I ever had to listen to it again."

She turned on the bench. Mr Darcy stood in the doorway. With arms crossed, he leaned against the door frame. A small smile played on his lips as he looked at her. He straightened and stepped into the room, walking slowly towards the pianoforte. Elizabeth rose from the bench and turned to face him.

Here was his likeness come to life. With a start she realized that he was an older version of the faded memory at Hatchard's. *Her* Mr Darcy.

"I find I do not mind the tune so much, especially when I have the pleasure of seeing *you* perform it." He was very close to her now. Elizabeth's heart raced as she gazed up into his face. He was *very* tall.

"Mr Darcy," she breathed. "Is it truly you?"

He smiled gently and reached up, cupping her cheek in his hand. "It is. Let us waste no more time."

He bent down, and his lips captured hers. His other hand snaked around her back, pressing her closer. Elizabeth's arms embraced his waist as she kissed him back, the pent-up emotions of months spilling out in that one act. When Darcy broke the kiss, he laid his cheek on the top of her head, enveloping her in his secure embrace. Elizabeth felt his lips touch her hair.

She pulled back slightly and looked up into his face. "You are here," she breathed, tears of joy glistening in her eyes. "It worked."

"Yes, my love," he said with great emotion. "It worked. It worked because of you. You saved me, Elizabeth. You saved both of us. Wickham's schemes ultimately failed, and I emerged from the whole ordeal unscathed. Georgiana suffered more, though... but I forget, you do not have the details."

He took her hand and led her to the sofa. Once seated, Darcy recounted the entirety of his history with George Wickham and the scoundrel's attempt to ruin his sister. "... and so, when I arrived at the

Lake House and read your letter, I was able to keep a level head about me when I found him with Georgiana. He... Wickham did not survive his fall."

Elizabeth leaned into his side and sighed. Darcy had never revealed the name of his former childhood friend. It stirred blurred memories of a militia officer of the same name, but the new, clearer memories overrode them. Unclear thoughts of the havoc tickled her mind, but she felt unsurprised to know it was the same man who had plagued Darcy's family.

"I am relieved that it ended well. But what of the intervening time—everything that has happened since? Your memories will differ from mine." Brief flashes of conversation, gatherings, and even a visit to Derbyshire flickered into her mind, though she had no clear recollection of them. "One version of events stands out in my memory, but it feels like it has been laid over another," she murmured. "How can I be sure what is real?"

Darcy turned towards her, his expression earnest. "This is real." His voice was husky and warm as he wrapped her in his embrace and ardently kissed her. Elizabeth melted into the kiss, reaching up and tangling her fingers through the soft curls that grazed his cravat.

A throat cleared from the doorway, and they broke apart.

"If I had known you would compromise Elizabeth within moments of your arrival, I might have vacated the house entirely." Charles regarded them with exaggerated gravity, though the teasing glint in his eyes hinted at the wide grin that followed. "It is about time," he continued. "I hope this means that there will be a wedding before the summer is out. The pair of you have been pining long enough!"

"I see no reason to delay," Elizabeth said immediately. She briefly wondered how the past had changed for her brother, but she resolved to think on it later.

Charles nodded. "I thought as much. Poor Elizabeth has been at sixes and sevens these past months, forced to endure the company of others, whilst she awaited you. Sort out the details and then come find me, eh, Darcy? I have Mr Bennet's part of the marriage articles in my study."

Elizabeth and Darcy exchanged smiles as Charles turned to leave. "Door open," he said over his shoulder. Sally sidled in just after his departure, sitting in a far corner as unobtrusively as possible.

Elizabeth curled up against Darcy. "How long must we wait?" she asked softly. He shifted slightly and pulled a common license from his pocket.

"Is tomorrow too soon?"

She reached up to touch his cheek. "Never. We have waited long enough."

Epilogue

Elizabeth soon realised she had much to learn. Many recollections surfaced in her mind, and careful enquiries confirmed they were all true. Darcy had indeed visited Netherfield with Bingley in the autumn of 1811. His overt enthusiasm upon meeting her at the assembly had deterred her from furthering their acquaintance, and despite his efforts, they had not reached an understanding before he was called away in November. A fire had broken out at Pemberley, demanding his immediate return.

The fragments of memory Elizabeth held suggested Darcy's attempts at courtship during his brief time in Hertfordshire had been tumultuous. He had attempted to keep himself aloof, afraid that his attentions might alter her future, that in doing so she would never send the letter that saved him. But her siren's call drove him to seek her company, confusing Elizabeth and driving her to keep her distance.

After his departure, Bingley's sisters had tried their best to convince their brother to abandon the estate, but dear Charles had resisted. He married Jane early in 1812. Elizabeth remembered the wedding clearly, though she could not recall if Darcy had been there. Charles insisted his friend or his brother-in-law had stood with him, but another family crisis had pulled Darcy away immediately after the wedding breakfast, leaving him no chance to speak to Elizabeth.

When she visited the Collinses at Hunsford during Easter, Lady Catherine subjected Elizabeth to her lamentations about the absence of her favourite nephew. Business matters had kept Darcy in London until after Elizabeth's departure from Kent.

The invitation to the Lake House at Ramsgate had come via letter when Charles wrote to Darcy about Jane's poor health. Mr Darcy had graciously offered the use of the Lake House for as long as needed, and the Bingleys happily accepted. Elizabeth travelled with them, just as she remembered, though at some point, she had left for a holiday with her London relations.

Darcy and Elizabeth both recalled seeing each other in Derbyshire whilst she was in the company of the Gardiners. The timing of the holiday had been ideal, as Jane had recovered much from of her illness, allowing Elizabeth to travel without worry for her sister. Her memories suggested Darcy had courted her in earnest during her stay, and he was on the verge of proposing when scandal separated them.

Lydia eloped with Mr Denny, a member of the militia whom she had met during the regiment's winter encampment at Meryton for the winter. They fled from Brighton whilst Lydia was staying with her particular friend, Mrs Forster, the wife of the regiment's colonel. Darcy found Denny and Lydia in London and ensured that they married.

After securing Lydia's marriage to Denny, Fate proved unkind once more, calling Darcy to Scotland to oversee the removal of an embezzling steward. The harsh winter months had trapped him in the north, and it was March before he had returned to Pemberley. Following that, small matters kept them apart until Darcy finally resolved to join the Bingleys and Elizabeth at the Lake House.

After Jane's tumultuous pregnancy and the birth of her children, they arranged a house party in Ramsgate. Darcy's sister and cousin confirmed their invitations, as did Elizabeth's sister, Mary. Thus, Georgiana and Colonel Fitzwilliam's presence in Ramsgate at this time was rewritten—not to await the end of a lease, but to enjoy the company of friends and family. During the evening, Darcy returned the music Elizabeth had found in the chair to his sister and encouraged her to retrieve their father's snuffbox from the hollow in the tree.

William and Margaret had not changed from what she remembered, and Elizabeth insisted she was still their favourite aunt and preferred playmate. Darcy was surprised and deeply honoured to learn that William had been named for him.

Darcy and Elizabeth married within a week of their reunion in Ramsgate. The ceremony was a simple affair, attended only by the Bingleys, Mary, Miss Darcy, and Colonel Fitzwilliam, yet it was beautiful. They stayed in Ramsgate for the rest of the summer, spending some time sequestered in a small cottage Darcy had leased for their wedding tour.

At times, it was hard to distinguish what was real from what was not. Once, Elizabeth awoke infuriated from a dream that seemed so vivid that she burst into tears upon waking. Thankfully, her dear husband was there to comfort her.

"What is troubling you?" he asked tenderly, drawing her into his arms.

"You insulted me." Elizabeth sniffled, wiping her nose with a handkerchief. "We were at an assembly in Meryton, and when Charles pressed you to dance, you called me tolerable and not handsome enough to tempt you!" Hurt filled her heart, and she buried her tear-streaked face in his chest. The irrational anger that threatened to overwhelm her stemmed from something deep within, leaving her to wonder whether it had been a memory or merely the product of a fatigued mind.

Her husband kissed her head and stroked her back soothingly. "We both know that I find you far more than *tolerable*. You are the handsomest woman of my acquaintance."

Elizabeth sighed and felt comforted. Darcy would never say such a thing. *Never.* She snuggled deeper into his embrace, and her husband held her until she drifted back to sleep.

Lady Catherine became incensed when Darcy married 'a country nobody' and vowed never to acknowledge Mrs Darcy. Elizabeth would not have minded much, except that her cousin Collins then forbade Charlotte from writing to her. Charlotte, however, paid him no heed and simply enclosed her letters in missives to her family, the Lucases, with a request to forward them to Pemberley or Darcy House.

Elizabeth *did* introduce Mary to Mr Blandishman, and the man's preoccupation with *her* quickly shifted in favour of her younger sister. After just three weeks of courtship, he proposed, and Mary accepted. Unlike Mr Collins, Mr Blandishman did not try to make Elizabeth feel regret for her lack of interest in him, instead thanking her for her good sense and for introducing him to his wife. The happy couple retreated to their estate after their wedding tour.

Jane and Charles purchased an estate not twenty miles from Pemberley when the twins turned a year old. Shortly after settling in, Jane discovered she was expecting again. This time, her health was far better, and she found she could enjoy the experience of carrying a child.

Lydia and Denny remained in the north for some time, frequently pestering the Bingleys and Darcys for funds. Jane was quick to offer aid, but Elizabeth was more reluctant, knowing that any help provided was likely to be squandered. Denny stayed quartered with a northern regiment for several years before he and his wife emigrated to the

Americas. They sent two or three letters in the first twelve months after their arrival, but no one heard from them thereafter. Elizabeth hoped the Dennys had built a successful life for themselves and avoided any misfortunes.

The year 1814 saw the birth of Bennet Charles Darcy. Mrs Bennet expressed her joy at having another grandson and congratulated Elizabeth on providing her husband with an heir so promptly. The Darcys would have three more children: two sons who, like their elder brother, inherited their father's striking looks and commanding stature, and a daughter who, in both appearance and temperament, was the very image of her mother. The children grew up much loved by their parents and enjoyed frequent company with their cousins, aunts, and uncles.

Kitty eventually found a husband after a successful season in Town. She came out in London with Georgiana Darcy, and the pair became the best of friends and closest confidantes. Both married and settled within an easy distance of each other, as happy in their lives as Jane and Elizabeth.

The Lake House remained much as it always had. After Bennet was born, the Darcys returned to Ramsgate, determined to continue their tradition of summers by the sea. Though still baffled by the strange events that brought them together, they persisted in their search to seek answers.

"It makes little sense," Elizabeth insisted. She and her husband sat in the Lake House's library, poring over the volumes they had gathered. "There is nothing here about any peculiar occurrences in the house."

"There was nothing at Pemberley, either," Darcy mused thoughtfully. "I thought surely we would uncover something in my ancestor's recordings."

"There was a volume missing from your grandmother's journals," Elizabeth reminded him. "An entire two-year span of memories—gone. I am certain the answers lie within that missing volume."

Her husband shrugged, resigned. "Alas, we cannot know for certain until we find it, and it does not seem to be here."

A discreet cough from the doorway drew their attention. Mr Smythe stood there, as composed and stoic as ever.

"If I may, sir, madam," he began, his tone formal yet hesitant. "There is something about the Lake House that you deserve to know."

Darcy gave him a nod, encouraging him to continue. Smythe entered the library and closed the door behind him. Crossing the room with measured steps, he came to stand before them, his hands clasped behind his back.

"Take a seat, Smythe," Darcy said, gesturing to a chair. He took it, perching on the edge of his seat nervously.

"You are aware," Smythe began hesitantly, "that this place possesses an unusual quality… it bridges time, connecting distinct moments. In fact, the Lake House holds a peculiar ability which enables those destined to find one another to do so. You may wonder how I have been able to serve both of you, unchanged, though separated by two years."

Smythe paused, clearing his throat and adjusting his cuffs. "The truth is, the house has chosen me, as it did those who came before me, as its steward. It allows me to exist within these walls across time. For me, 1810 and 1812 are not separate but rather intertwined. I have moved between them, ensuring that the letters you exchanged reached their rightful hands at the precise moment necessary." He looked at his master and mistress, gauging their reactions to his startling revelation before continuing.

"There is a hidden post box, built into the wall behind the painting of Antony Lake—your many-greats grandfather—near the entry. That post box serves as the focal point of the connexion—the bridge that allowed your letters to traverse time."

Darcy's expression was incredulous but not disbelieving. "Go on," choked Darcy, hoarse with emotion.

Smythe nodded and resumed. "This is not a power I wield, but a responsibility bestowed upon me by the house itself. It has guided me, as it did those in my family before me, just as it guided your letters. The house's purpose is to unite individuals—those in whom it senses a bond yet unrealised, a couple destined to be together in life, whose connexion transcends the ordinary. Why the house does this, I cannot say with certainty, but I believe it senses something unique in these individuals, driving it to unite them.

In your case, the House spared Miss Darcy from potential tragedy, and you, sir, from a far graver fate—death at the hands of that vermin, Wickham. *My* role was to see that you and Mrs Darcy came together and to safeguard the connexion the house had forged between you."

Smythe smiled, a rare sight that startled Elizabeth to her core. *How long have I attempted to elicit such an expression?*

"Now that you are married," the butler continued, "and your family members are safe, the house has served its purpose for you. The post box will remain dormant now, its work complete, until it is once more called upon to help other individuals destined to cross the Lake House's threshold, just as it helped the two of you. I shall return to my usual duties, grateful to have played a part in your story, leaving the next chapter to be written by a future generation. Know that your bond is one the house itself deemed worthy—a truth most extraordinary. As for the missing journal, Mrs. Amelia Darcy left it in my great-grandmother's care. I have it if you desire to read it."

Despite their butler's assurances, as they grew older, Mr and Mrs Darcy often wondered whether all that Fate—or perhaps Providence—had brought upon them had truly unfolded as they remembered. Yet, when doubts crept in, they would retrieve a small wooden box, adorned with a brass clasp and hinges, and carved with delicate lavender blossoms on its lid. Inside lay a year's worth of letters, tangible proof that their love story had spanned the reaches of time. Never would they forget or deny the events that had shaped their lives, and they would remain forever grateful for the unseen force that had intervened and given their love the chance to flourish.

I hope you enjoyed *The Lake House at Ramsgate*! This Pride and Prejudice variation was inspired by one of my favorite movies, *The Lake House.* Check it out of you have not seen it yet!

Be sure to check out my other books. I have a soft spot for redemption stories, so if that's a favorite trope of yours, take a look at my other books! Find them at Amazon.com!

<u>MJ Stratton Books</u>

Thank you for reading!

Other Books by MJ Stratton

Note: Books with an asterisk are redemption stories

Darcy and Lizzy Variations:

A Far Better Prospect**

When Given Good Principles**

No Less Than Any Other

The Lake House at Ramsgate

Thwarted

To Marry for Love

Love Unfeigned

Other Stories:

The Redemption of Lydia Wickham**

Catherine Called Kitty**

Mary, Marry? Quite Contrary!**

Charming Caroline**

Charmed

From Another Perspective

Crossroads

Variations from Jane Austen's other works

What Ought to Have Been**

Thank you for reading!

Thank You!

I truly hope you enjoyed this book. If you loved it and would like to let me know, or even if you didn't, I would love to hear about it! Be assured, I read all my reviews on:

Amazon.com

Goodreads.com

Reach out wherever you like, or feel free to contact me at

author.mjstratton@gmail.com

Follow me on Facebook!

https://www.facebook.com/AuthorMJStratton

Acknowledgements

A special thank you to everyone (betas, editors, ARC participants) who helped me along with this book. A special thanks to Marie, Gratia, Rebecca, and Sunsette for your efforts to help make this book free of error.

Thanks to Summer Hanford for her efforts with editing, paperback covers, and moral support. Your expertise has made me a better writer, and my books are always more polished after you've had your way with them, and this one is no different! How you manage to spot all the little inconsistencies astounds me. But most importantly for your friendship.

Thank you to Pemberley Darcy for the spectacular cover design!

And, as always, thank you to my darling husband, who has supported me through it all, especially when it came to finding time to write while still being a wife and mom. This book was your idea in the first place, and I think it turned out very well.

About The Author

MJ Stratton's love affair with Jane Austen began at sixteen, thanks to a much-beloved aunt who introduced her to *Pride and Prejudice*. That fateful moment led to an insatiable passion for Austenesque fiction, sealing her destiny as both a reader and a writer. After nearly a decade of beta reading and editing for others, MJ took the plunge into publishing her own works in 2022.

A lifelong enthusiast of reading, learning, and all things bookish, MJ balances her time between crafting Regency tales, tending to her garden, and sewing her way through creative projects. She shares her small-town life with her husband, four lively children, and cats who firmly believes they are the true masters of the household.

When she's not writing or wrangling her feline overlords, MJ can usually be found lost in a book, researching obscure historical facts, or daydreaming about her next story.

Printed in Dunstable, United Kingdom